The Rural Spirit

The Rural Spirit

Language of the Earth and Sky

Compiled by

Mervyn Wilson

COLLINS

8 Grafton Street, London W1

William Collins Sons & Co. Ltd
London · Glasgow · Sydney · Auckland
Toronto · Johannesburg

First published in Great Britain in 1990 by
Collins Religious Division,
Part of the Collins Publishing Group
8 Grafton Street, London W1X 3LA

Printed and bound in Great Britain

CONTENTS

From *Paradise Lost*

                          Let th' earth
Put forth the verdant grass, herb yielding seed,
And fruit tree yielding fruit after her kind;
Whose seed is in herself upon the earth.
He scarce had said, when the bare earth, till then
Desert and bare, unsightly, unadorn'd,
Brought forth the tender grass, whose verdure clad
Her universal face with pleasant green;
Then herbs of every leaf, that sudden flow'r'd
Op'ning their various colours, and made gay
Her bosom smelling sweet: and these scarce blown,
Forth flourish'd thick the clust'ring vine, forth crept
The swelling gourd, up stood the corny reed
Embattel'd in her field; and th' humble shrub,
And bush with frizzled hair implicit: last
Rose, as in dance, the stately trees, and spread
Their branches hung with copious fruit, or gemm'd
Their blossoms: with high woods the hills were crown'd;
With tufts the valleys and each fountain side,
With borders long the rivers: that earth now
Seem'd like to heav'n, a seat where Gods might dwell,
Or wander with delight, and love to haunt
Her sacred shades:

JOHN MILTON (1608–1674)

INTRODUCTION

In Bermondsey between the wars, surrounded by brick and smoke, with cramped houses, factories and people everywhere, the local council appointed a Beautification Committee. They established parks and planted trees and flowers. The local Rector even published a small book called *Daffodils in Bermondsey*. The aim was that the people of the neighbourhood might retain something of the peacefulness and love of natural beauty which their ancestors had known in the rural setting before the shift of population to the industrialised cities in the last century. Often it is the urban experience that heightens our awareness of the rural. We have begun to realise that the land, cultivated and wild, the natural world, the sea and the sky are as important to the human soul as the social life of the city.

This collection of writings illustrates mankind's awareness of and searching after the spiritual in, through and beyond the natural world. Today there are many active environmentalists and a general concern for green issues and the future of the planet. What I have tried to do is assemble passages which place these issues in a larger and longer tradition.

Although this collection is inevitably personal, I hope other readers will find it in something that stands as an objective frame of reference. Most of the passages reveal a Christian origin and faith. To the Christian a love of nature on its own is a lopsided enthusiasm and is ultimately disappointing. There is also a Lord of Nature. Human dominion on its own is as much a force of destruction as for good and the Christian accepts that he is only a steward, however privileged.

The anthology progresses from the seen to the unseen. We are moved by beauty to look beyond. Wonder at creation leads to a search for what underlies it. Individually I hope pieces will stand up to being read aloud since that was one of my criteria for inclusion. Also I hope that they will gain from association, for example the pieces by St Augustine, John Clare and Thomas Merton which all describe the language of nature.

1

Although the selection is mine and much of it reflects my reading and taste, the genesis lay with the Rural Theology Association, whose members several years ago resolved to collect prose and poetry to illustrate life in the country and the rural spirit. Here I would like particularly to acknowledge a debt to Leslie Francis who has given much advice, to Tony Hodgson, Martin Marix-Evans and Tim Cawkwell with whom the project has been discussed, to June Bernstein and others who suggested pieces for inclusion and to the late Bill Miller and my wife Margaret who have helped with the production.

MERVYN WILSON

The World Around Us

The World Around Us

What is it that we find so refreshing when we go for a walk in the countryside? There is a sort of pleasure in crumbling the earth under one's feet and another in walking on grass. Perhaps the eye is caught by a little pond or a tree just breaking into leaf. On a spring afternoon the sun breaks through for a moment, then hailstones hit coldly. A duck flies overhead.

The passages in this section mostly describe what anyone might see and some of the feelings and thoughts such sights can evoke. I have often found my appreciation enriched by someone else's remembered reflection or the odd snatch of a poem. T. S. Eliot's line, "Dawn points and another day prepares for heat and silence" has often come into my mind while walking in my garden early on a summer morning.

What's in Earth?

from A Word in Season

While you're walking along, do you ever wonder
What's beneath you, deep down under?

Down below there's a lot going on
Under the path that we're walking along:
Little roots, big roots, tunnelling moles,
Rabbits in burrows and worms in their holes.

While you're walking along, do you ever wonder
What's beneath you, deep down under?

Is there coal down there where the miners toil?
Or salt perhaps. Or clay. Or oil.
Have you ever thought what the earth is giving
To make us happy and keep us living?

ANITA HEWETT (1918–)

To an Earthworm

from A Word in Season

You worm!
Despised of man,
Trodden underfoot,
Cast to the hungry robin, tempting him to stay,
Or yet ignored, as spade bites deeper into frosty earth.

And yet . . .
Beneath the moving earth
Where noisy revolution
Is silent
To deaf man
You work your works with patience
And with zeal.

Piercing, you cast the earth behind you,
Miniature torrents follow in your stead,
Life-giving
And renewing.
Soil breaks on soil and earth begins to breathe.
Whilst all the myriad creatures aid your part;
Releasing life
And hope for eager roots.

You worm!
Despised of man in ignorant conceit.
But coveted by earth, feeding on your labours
And offering its unity to Him.

DONALD HILTON (1932–)

Night Wind

Darkness like midnight from the sobbing woods
Clamours with dismal tidings of the rain
Roaring as rivers breaking loose in floods
To spread and foam and deluge all the plain
The cotter listens at his door again
Half doubting wether it be floods or wind
And through the thickening darkness looks affraid
Thinking of roads that travel has to find
Through nights black depths in dangers garb arrayed
And the loud glabber round the flaze soon stops
When hushed to silence by the lifted hand
Of fearing dame who hears the noise in dread
And thinks a deluge comes to drown the land
Nor dares she go to bed untill the tempest drops

JOHN CLARE (1793–1864)

Morning Wind

There's more than music in this early wind
Awaking like a bird refreshed from sleep
And joy what Adam might in eden find
When he with angels did communion keep
It breaths all balm and insence from the sky
Blessing the husbandman with freshening powers
Joys manna from its wings doth fall and lie
Harvests for early wakers with the flowers
The very grass in joys devotion moves
Cowslaps in adoration and delight
This way and that bow to the breath they love
Of the young winds that with the dew pearls play
Till smoaking chimneys sicken the young light
And feelings fairey visions fade away

JOHN CLARE (1793–1864)

Cloud Shapes

from Modern Painters

How is a cloud outlined? Granted whatever you choose to ask, concerning its material, or its aspect, its loftiness and luminousness, – how of its limitation? What hews it into a heap, or spins it into a web? Cold is usually shapeless, I suppose, extending over large spaces equally, or with gradual diminution. You cannot have, in the open air, angles, and wedges, and coils, and cliffs of cold. Yet the vapour stops suddenly, sharp and steep as a rock, or thrusts itself across the gates of heaven in likeness of a brazen bar; or braids itself in and out, and across and across, like a tissue of tapestry; or falls into ripples like sand; or into waving shreds and tongues, hammered, whirled, as the potter's clay? By what hands is the incense of the sea built up into domes of marble?

JOHN RUSKIN (1819–1900)

Relating to the Sky

from Spacious Skies

Sky and weather are not so abstract that we can't develop a relationship to them. In the obvious sense this means a sharing of information wherein sky passes on clues about weather wisdom and we assess them in the light of scientific fact and personal experience. An ensuing familiarity with sky then gives us many other, less obvious, practical benefits like a keener sense of awareness of nature and a growing recognition of how inseparable we really are from our environment.

Watching the sky raises our appreciation for science in general by bringing it directly into our everyday experiences. As a result, we begin to appreciate clouds for their own sake. Those foolish notions that 'good weather' means clear days and blue skies are soon dispelled and replaced with a more realistic response to weather. Can you imagine all those people who step out of bed and permit their thoughts and moods to slump just because the day is overcast! Even the seemingly dull overcast sky has its special offering of windswept fragments, scented moistness, soothing greys and quiet light to share with us. Discovering our environment and getting to know it better makes us want to see the same familiar skies over and over, but always in search of new experiences and the surprises they harbour.

Because of the complexity of sky, it is impossible to apply many rules to being a critical sky observer. Instead, it is better to rely on our other skills to provide a gradual, thorough understanding of this subject. Despite rigorous methods and a technological garb, science has no monopoly on truth or fact. We ought to shrug off the intimidation of expertise and the convenience of ready-made answers and become the authors of more personal and relevant associations with the world around us. This by no means implies the abandonment of present scientific methods that test and prove our notions, but rather their supplementation with an alternative way of assessing information. Through the application of pattern recognition, relational thinking, and an interactive awareness as they pertain to sky, we develop our intuitive abilities. These abilities are better able to cope with the meaning of things in the larger context of life, and make each one of us participants in the advancements of scientific knowledge.

Our relationship to sky is one-to-one, and from it we learn to see things differently. You can't be a good observer of sky, or anything else for that matter, unless you give yourself to the subject, open up to it, let it flow through you. This is much like spiritually centered living in that you allow sky to live within and express itself through you. To really see things in their fullness we need to become a part of what we're looking at.

Sky is a convenient, readily available way to enjoy ourselves. And in the process, we become less detached from our surroundings. We begin to participate and appreciate the things we are exposed to rather than passively enduring their presence. In doing so, we take another step towards the reclamation of a nearly lost heritage in which personal responsibilities have been supplanted by collective indifference.

RICHARD SCORER and ARJEN VERKAIK

Polar Sun

O sun!
Permit us to pass our days prosperously;
Do not abandon us in the future,
Until the warm spring breezes come!

ANONYMOUS

The Faithful River

from The Mirror of the Sea

The estuaries of rivers appeal strongly to an adventurous imagination. This appeal is not always a charm, for there are estuaries of a particularly dispiriting ugliness: lowlands, mudflats, or perhaps barren sandhills without beauty of form or amenity of aspect, covered with a shabby and scanty vegetation conveying the impression of poverty and uselessness. Sometimes such an ugliness is merely a repulsive mask. A river whose estuary resembles a breach in a sand rampart may flow through a most fertile country. But all the estuaries of great rivers have their fascination, the attractiveness of an open portal. Water is friendly to man. The ocean, a part of Nature farthest removed in the unchangeableness and majesty of its might from the spirit of mankind, has ever been a friend to the enterprising nations of the earth. And of all the elements this is the one to which men have always been prone to trust themselves, as if its immensity held a reward as vast as itself.

From the offing the open estuary promises every possible fruition to adventurous hopes. That road open to enterprise and courage invites the explorer of coasts to new efforts towards the fulfilment of great expectations. The commander of the first Roman galley must have looked with an intense absorption upon the estuary of the Thames as he turned the beaked prow of his ship to the westward under the brow of the North Foreland. The estuary of the Thames is not beautiful; it has no noble features, no romantic grandeur of aspect, no smiling geniality; but it is wide open, spacious, inviting, hospitable at the first glance, with a strange air of mysteriousness which lingers about it to this very day.

JOSEPH CONRAD (1857–1924)

The Desert

from *The Gobi Desert*

An aerial view of the Desert of Gobi on a midsummer day would show a burning arid waste of dunes interspersed with monotonous rolling expanses of gravel and crossed by occasional ridges of high mountains whose foothills dwindle to low rocky mounds. The whole plain is shadeless and exposed to scorching heat under a pitiless sun. All living creatures seek shelter from its fierce rays and the roads are deserted, for the reverberation of heat makes travel almost impossible.

By night it is quite otherwise, and as darkness falls the desert quickens into life. Scorching heat gives way to a sudden chill which rises from the ground and strikes the traveller with a cold impact which makes him lift his head to catch the warmer upper stratum of the air as a relief from that too palpable cold. Soon that layer too will be permeated by the chill, and he will wrap a sheepskin coat around him in an endeavour to keep warm.

At this hour the observer would see caravans emerge from all the oasis inns. Not only humans but innumerable small animals and insects come from their hiding-places as soon as darkness falls. All through the hours of heat they have slept in the tunnelled world which they have burrowed for themselves a few feet underground, and of which the openings are on the sheltered side of many a tiny sand-mound, blown up round the foot of a tuft of camel-thorn or of a low bush of scrub. All through the night the little live things move ceaselessly, silently and invisibly over the sand, and only by chance does a traveller become aware of their presence; after sunrise, however, he sees the sand patterned with all kinds of beautiful markings left by small rodents, beetles, centipedes and other insects which scuttle back to their sleeping-quarters with the first ray of sunshine.

Near the oases an observer might see slinking forms of

wolves prowling vigilantly lest a goat or a child should wander from the shelter of the houses, and when some tired beast lags behind the caravan the dark forms gather from all sides to snatch a share of the spoil. Other sinister forms sometimes crouch behind rocks or in gullies – evil men waiting for lonely pedestrians or for some cart which has ventured unattached over the desert waste. The robbers hide themselves at those points on the route where caravans going north must pass just after sunset and where others, travelling south, come in shortly before daylight, for during the grey, twilight hours they will be unnoticed among the elusive shadows.

In the dry desert air the sky becomes a beautiful background for the brilliant stars which hang clear, showing themselves as shining orbs and never creating the illusion of lights twinkling through holes in a curtain, as is the case in dull and murky climes. The Milky Way is not the whitish haze seen in Western skies, but like a phosphorescent shower of myriad spots of light. Night travellers are great star-gazers, and look out over an uninterrupted line of horizon to skies which are always cloudless. The clearness and watchfulness of each planet suggests a personal and friendly interest toward the wayfarer, and Venus has served as beacon to many a caravan crossing doubtful stages.

Of starlight in the desert, Lawrence of Arabia writes: "The brilliant stars cast about us a false light, not illumination, but rather a transparency of air, lengthening slightly the shadow below each stone and making a diffused greyness of the ground." Desert men, accustomed all their lives to that most subtle of all light diffusions, walk freely, even on rough ground, with no other illuminant. The moon, also, is more self-revealing than in heavier atmospheres, and never pretends to be merely a silver sickle or a cradle swinging in the void. She shows her full-orbed sphere, hanging in space, with a varying portion of brilliance outlining her darkened luminosity. With the rising of the moon the desert takes on its most captivating appearance, and through the long hours while she travels from one side of the horizon to the other she has her own way with human imagination, softening all the austere outlines and investing the barest formations with subtle charm. She is a mistress of magic and with one touch can turn the wilderness into a dream world.

MILDRED CABLE with FRANCESCA FRENCH

Wilderness and Wet

What would the world be, once bereft
Of wet and of wildness? Let them be left,
O let them be left, wildness and wet;
Long live the weeds and the wilderness yet.

GERARD MANLEY HOPKINS (1844–1889)

The Wildwood

from Gothic Ramblings in Somerset

Gone for the most part are the great forests of England, and looking back they seem to us romantic places, every forest in some sort a forest adventurous, where a knight, if he were good liver, might like Sir Badgemagus read words upon a woodland cross, and find by the way a holy herb that was the sign of the Sangreal; where you might meet a giant under a holly tree, or see four queens on white mules, under their canopy of green silk borne by four knights, happen upon Sir Lancelot asleep in an apple tree's shade, while upon another tree hung shields of many vanquished knights, who must languish in prison till Sir Lancelot come. Or else we think of them as merry woods, peopled for us by Shakespeare, here Robin Goodfellow impishly laughing at lovers from behind a tree, there some fallen courtier stringing his bow in search of game. Or else with Herrick we have been amaying, and come rejoicing home, laden with flowering thorn. We have never wandered night bound in the wood, praying we might meet no worse adventure than to stumble upon the hut of some charcoal burner in the dawn, where we might break our fast on homely fare and be set right on our way by the rough dweller in the wood. We may lament at times the passing of the great woods that once spread far and wide, that have vanished with the taming of our land. We have remembered the enchantment of the forest, and nigh forgotten its terror.

For centuries after the Christianisation of our land, witches resorted more especially to the woods for their evil rites, as if old gods of fear like a conquered people had taken to the woods as their last refuge. There were still fierce beasts in the thickets. Langland as late as Edward III's reign speaks of the ravages of "bores and brokkes" upon Piers Ploughman's crops. Wolves still lurked in the remoter forests down to Tudor times; I doubt if more than the memory of wolves lingered in our Somerset woods when this carving was made, but it was a far more recent memory than gave wolves a lair in a copse upon Brent Knoll when as a child I passed downhill at night, the pine trees sighing in the wind, and whatever light of the stars might be on the fields the entrance to the copse lay deep in shadow. Had any farm dog bayed upon the hill, at ten years old I should have run down Saddleclose as if a pack of wolves had been at my heels.

FREDA DERRICK

Trees

from Afoot in England

I could on each recurring November have such an afternoon
ride, with that autumnal glory in the trees. Sometimes, seeing
the road before me carpeted with pure yellow, I said to myself,
now I am coming to elms; but when the road shone red and
russet-gold before me I knew it was overhung by beeches. But
the oak is the common tree in this place, and from every high
point on the road I saw far before me and on either hand the
woods and copses all a tawny yellow gold – the hue of the
dying oak leaf. The tall larches were lemon-yellow, and when
growing among tall pines produced a singular effect. Best of
all was it where beeches grew among the firs, and the low sun
on my left hand shining through the wood gave the coloured
translucent leaves an unimaginable splendour. This was the
very effect which men, inspired by a sacred passion, had sought
to reproduce in their noblest works – the Gothic cathedral and
church, its dim interior lit by many-coloured stained glass. The
only choristers in these natural fanes were the robins and the
small lyrical wren; but on passing through the rustic village of
Wolverton I stopped for a couple of minutes to listen to the
lively strains of a cirl bunting among some farm buildings.

· W. H. HUDSON (1841–1922)

The Riches of the Rainforest

from The Greening of the Church

Little wonder, then, that the richness and splendour of the forest is not appreciated by many people. Sad to say, the majority of teachers and educators – even those who promote nationalism – fit into this category. They are ignorant about the forests and place little value on their preservation. Because of their lack of knowledge they are unable to communicate the wonders of this amazing world to their students or to the population at large. Except for the tribal people, who are at home there, and the handful of scientists who are deepening our knowledge of the rainforests, most people see them as dangerous, dark and forbidding places full of poisonous snakes and wild animals ready to pounce on human beings and devour them.

One reason for the bad press is the stereotype image of the rainforest. Here man is pitted against nature. The hero is often portrayed as a Tarzan-like figure battling against the green hell of the jungle which is reaching out its clawing tendrils to encircle and defeat him. Anyone with the slightest knowledge of the rainforest knows that this image is totally false, yet it is deeply ingrained in modern estern consciousness. Hollywood regularly shows us Rambo figures wreaking havoc on the forest. But even our everyday language betrays us: we speak of the "law of the jungle" as if death and destruction were the primary realities there. On the contrary, the rainforest – like every other ecosystem – is made up of a complex web of co-operative and symbiotic relationships.

SEAN McDONAGH

Wonder of the World

Job 37: 21–24; 38: 4–11, 33–35; 39: 26–30

"And now men cannot look on the light
  when it is bright in the skies
  when the wind has passed and cleared them.
Out of the north comes golden splendour;
  God is clothed with terrible majesty.
The Almighty – we cannot find him;
  he is great in power and justice,
  and abundant righteousness he will not violate.
Therefore men fear him;
  he does not regard any who are wise in their own conceit.'

Where were you when I laid the foundation of the earth?
  Tell me, if you have understanding.
Who determined its measurements – surely you know!
  Or who stretched the line upon it?
On what were its bases sunk,
  or who laid its cornerstone,
when the morning stars sang together,
  and all the sons of God shouted for joy?

Or who shut in the sea with doors,
  when it burst forth from the womb;
when I made clouds its garment,
  and thick darkness its swaddling band,
and prescribed bounds for it,
  and set bars and doors,
and said, 'Thus far shall you come, and no farther,
  and here shall your proud waves be stayed'?

Do you know the ordinances of the heavens?
  Can you establish their rule on the earth?
  Can you lift up your voice to the clouds,

that a flood of waters may cover you?
Can you send forth lightnings, that they may go
    and say to you, 'Here we are'?

Is it by your wisdom that the hawk soars,
    and spreads his wings toward the south?
Is it at your command that the eagle mounts up
    and makes his nest on high?
On the rock he dwells and makes his home
    in the fastness of the rocky crag.
Thence he spies out the prey;
    his eyes behold it afar off.
His young ones suck up blood;
    and where the slain are, there is he.''

The Study of Butterflies

from The Reality of God

Then there was the interest, after having caught and bred the Common Swallow-Tail in England, of finding the Scarce Swallow-Tail, most common throughout the Tyrol, and of comparing the two, and this without a moment's doubt that what I then found they had in common was as real, as little the work of my own mind, as what differentiated them. It was also a keen delight to find in the valleys of the Dolomites, as it were a glorified White in the gorgeous Apollo butterfly, with its largely transparent wings and the rich circles of red and black upon them. And, when I was given large collections of unmounted butterflies from Brazil, I found there relatives near and distant to our Red Admiral, Peacock, and especially to our Purple Emperor. And, in regard to all these natural groupings, I could not doubt that I was in face, not of constructions of my mind, but of facts objectively existent. I found that the characteristics of the groups varied within themselves and ended with the ending of the group, not only as regarded the appearance of the complete insect, but also as regarded the characteristics of the caterpillars and of the eggs, and even of the scales which covered the wings of the animal in its final stage. It is possible roughly to construct a system of the various genera of butterflies from the shape of their respective scales alone. This assuredly cannot be a conception or hypothesis of our minds, but has simply to be taken as a fact quite distinct from these apprehending minds of ours.

I trust the reader sees what I am driving at – a universal law of existence. True, there exist realities which can be termed *individual*, as compared with the realities of the characteristics they have in common with others of the same species; but, after all, the individual nowhere exists, among finite beings at least, as individual pure and simple. Such a pure individual finite being would be too utterly repulsive, if it did exist, for us to succeed in giving it that attention and affection without which there is no accurate knowledge of anything whatsoever. The higher a real being is in the scale of existence, the more numerous, the more active and powerful, are its relations with other realities.

BARON FRIEDRICH VON HUGEL (1852–1925)

The Coney at home

from Wild Animals at Home

No one has ever yet found the home nest of the Calling Hare. It is so securely hidden under rocks, and in galleries below rocks, that all attempts to dig it out have thus far failed. I know of several men, not to mention Bears, Badgers, Wolverines, and Grizzlies, who have essayed to unearth the secret of the Coney's inner life. Following on the trail of a Coney that bleated derisively at me near Pagoda Peak, Colorado, I began at once to roll rocks aside in an effort to follow him home to his den. The farther I went the less satisfaction I found. The uncertain trail ramified more and more as I laboured. Once or twice from far below me I heard a mocking squeak that spurred me on, but that too, ceased. When about ten tons of rock had been removed I was baffled. There were half a dozen possible lines of continuation, and while I paused to wipe the "honest sweat" from my well-meaning brow, I heard behind me the "weak", "weak", of my friend as though giving his estimate of my resolution, and I descried him – I suppose the same – on a rock point like a moss-bump against the sky-line away to the left. Only, one end of the moss-bump moved a little each time a squeak was cast upon the air. I had not time to tear down the whole mountain, so I did as my betters, the Bears and Badgers have done before me, I gave it up. I had at least found out why the Coney avoids the pleasant prairie and the fertile banks, and I finished with a new and profounder understanding of the Scripture text which says in effect, "As for the Coney, his safe refuge is in the rocks."

ERNEST THOMPSON SETON (1860–1946)

27

Magical Light

I would agree that there are in other lands more majestic scenes of rugged cliffs and snow-topped mountains than can be seen in England, but for homely restful beauty and joy, the English countryside is the fairest scenery on earth I know. And on Whit Monday I feasted my eyes on it; the sweet rise and fall of rolling woods, the shimmering lines of rolling downs, the dreamy distances of brooding hills on the borderland of Wales. There was breeze enough to move the fields of young springing corn, and so to change the pattern of the shades of green as the wind swept along the hillside. The splendour of spreading beech trees and the shadows of the tufted elms all wove their spell of beauty. Patient cows stood beside the silent pools, and half-grown lambs scampered away to frolic or to seek security beside their mothers. The sun's transforming power was everywhere. Its warmth was welcome enough, but the magic of its light transformed the scene. It was easy to understand the ancient religion of sun worshippers, but more comforting to know the Lord and Giver of Light and Life and the Light of the World. The perception of beauty brings an inner content; and as we learn to recognise beauty in simple and common-place things, we begin to gain insight into the ordering of a world whose Creator and Perfecter is Beauty, Truth and Goodness.

JOHN LEONARD WILSON (1897–1970)

Alone in the Wilderness

Alone in the Wilderness

Is it ever possible to be completely alone? Perhaps not except on the polar ice, in the endless desert or in the quietest parts of the Pacific Ocean. Yet even there it is only humans who are absent. In all of us there is a need to get away from our daily cares and worries, to seek peace, quiet and solitude.

This selection is however not chiefly concerned with the delights of the solitary rambler. There is also another solitude which brings with it a sense of isolation and an oppressive sense of separation. We sometimes use the word alienation as though somehow we have become strangers in what was once our home. Old relationships have gone dead on us. Old consolations in which we sought refuge have lost their power. The light seems to have gone out of the sun. As Wordsworth wrote, "There hath passed away a glory from the earth".

Lost Youth

No, never again, like you, graceful melodious girl-like,
My limbs will not carry me. O blow, blow that I might be
Like the bird who skims o'er the foam-flowered waves carefree
With the halcyons, bird of the sapphire springtime sea.

ALCMAN (c. 630 B.C.)

Desolation

Isaiah 24: 4–10; 34: 9–15

The earth mourns and withers,
  the world languishes and withers;
  the heavens languish together with the earth.
The earth lies polluted
  under its inhabitants;
for they have transgressed the laws,
  violated the statutes,
  broken the everlasting covenant.
Therefore a curse devours the earth,
  and its inhabitants suffer for their guilt;
therefore the inhabitants of the earth are scorched,
  and few men are left.
The wine mourns,
  the vine languishes,
  all the merry-hearted sigh.
The mirth of the timbrels is stilled,
  the noise of the jubilant has ceased,
  the mirth of the lyre is stilled.
No more do they drink wine with singing;
  strong drink is bitter to those who drink it.
The city of chaos is broken down,
  every house is shut up so that none can enter.

And the streams of Edom shall be turned into pitch,
  and her soil into brimstone;
  her land shall become burning pitch.
Night and day it shall not be quenched;
  its smoke shall go up for ever.
From generation to generation it shall lie waste;
  none shall pass through it for ever and ever.
But the hawk and the porcupine shall possess it,
  the owl and the raven shall dwell in it.

He shall stretch the line of confusion over it,
   and the plummet of chaos over its nobles.
They shall name it No Kingdom There,
   and all its princes shall be nothing.
Thorns shall grow over its strongholds,
   nettles and thistles in its fortresses.
It shall be the haunt of jackals,
   an abode for ostriches.
And wild beasts shall meet with hyenas,
   the satyr shall cry to his fellow;
yea, there shall the night hag alight,
   and find for herself a resting place.
There shall the owl nest and lay
   and hatch and gather her young in her shadow;
yea, there shall the kites be gathered,
   each one with her mate.

The Sleeping Lord

Yet he sleeps on
                              very deep in his slumber:
how long has be been the sleeping lord?
are the clammy ferns
                              his rustling vallance
does the buried rowan
                              ward him from evil, or
does he ward the tanglewood
                              and the denizens of the wood
are the stunted oaks his gnarled guard
                              or are their knarred limbs
strong with his sap?
Do the small black horses
                              grass on the hunch of his shoulders?
are the hills his couch
                              or is he the couchant hills?
Are the slumbering valleys
                              him in slumber
                              are the still undulations
the still limbs of him sleeping?
Is the configuration of the land
                              the furrowed body of the lord
are the scarred ridges
                              his dented greaves
do the trickling gullies
                              yet drain his hog-wounds?
Does the land wait the sleeping lord
                              or is the wasted land
that very lord who sleeps?

DAVID JONES (1895–)

35

Friend or Enemy

Thou art indeed just, Lord, if I contend
With thee; but, sir, so what I plead is just.
Why do sinners' ways prosper? and why must
Disappointment all I endeavour end?
  Wert thou my enemy, O thou my friend,
How wouldst thou worse, I wonder, than thou dost
Defeat, thwart me? Oh, the sots and thralls of lust
Do in spare hours more thrive than I that spend,
Sir, life upon thy cause. See, banks and brakes
Now, leavèd how thick I lacèd they are again
With fretty chervil, look, and fresh wind shakes
Them; birds build – but not I build; no, but strain,
Time's eunuch, and not breed one work that wakes.
Mine, O thou lord of life, send my roots rain.

GERARD MANLEY HOPKINS (1844–1889)

Drowning

Psalm 69: 1–3

Save me, O God: for the waters are come in, even unto my soul.

I stick fast in the deep mire, where no ground is: I am come into deep waters, so that the floods run over me.

I am weary of crying; my throat is dry: my sight faileth me for waiting so long upon my God.

Switzerland Defiled

from The Queen of the Air

This first day of May, 1869, I am writing where my work was begun thirty-five years ago, within sight of the snows of the higher Alps. In that half of the permitted life of man, I have seen strange evil brought upon every scene that I best loved, or tried to make beloved by others. The light which once flushed those pale summits with its rose at dawn, and purple at sunset, is now umbered and faint; the air which once inlaid the clefts of all their golden crags with azure is now defiled with languid coils of smoke, belched from worse than volcanic fires; their very glacier waves are ebbing, and their snows fading, as if Hell had breathed on them; the waters that once sank at their feet into crystalline rest are now dimmed and foul, from deep to deep, and shore to shore. These are no careless words – they are accurately – horribly – true. I know what the Swiss lakes were; no pool of Alpine fountain at its source was clearer. This morning, on the Lake of Geneva, at half a mile from the beach, I could scarcely see my oar-blade a fathom deep.

JOHN RUSKIN (1819–1900)

Not in Us

The injured elements say, "Not in us";
And night and day, ocean and continent,
Fire, plant and mineral say, "Not in us";
And haughtily return us stare for stare.
For we invade them impiously for gain;
We devastate them unreligiously,
And coldly ask their pottage, not their love.
Therefore they shove us from them, yield to us
Only what to our griping toil is due;
But the sweet affluence of love and song,
The rich results of the divine consents
Of man and earth, of world beloved and lover,
The nectar and ambrosia are withheld;
And in the midst of spoils and slaves, we thieves
And pirates of the universe, shut out
Daily to a more thin and outward rind,
Turn pale and starve. Therefore, to our sick eyes,
The stunted trees look sick, the summer short,
Clouds shade the sun, which will not tan our hay,
And nothing thrives to reach its natural term;
And life, shorn of its venerable length,
Even at its greatest space is a defeat.

RALPH WALDO EMERSON (1803–1882)

Wilderness Replanted

Isaiah 41: 6–8, 17–20

A voice says, "Cry!"
   And I said, "What shall I cry?"
All flesh is grass,
   and all its beauty is like the flower of the field.
The grass withers, the flower fades,
   when the breath of the LORD blows upon it;
   surely the people is grass.
The grass withers, the flower fades;
   but the word of our God will stand for ever.

When the poor and needy seek water,
   and there is none,
   and their tongue is parched with thirst,
I the LORD will answer them,
   I the God of Israel will not forsake them.
I will open rivers on the bare heights,
   and fountains in the midst of the valleys;
I will make the wilderness a pool of water,
   and the dry land springs of water.
I will put in the wilderness the cedar,
   the acacia, the myrtle, and the olive;
I will set in the desert the cypress,
   the plane and the pine together;
that men may see and know,
   may consider and understand together,
that the hand of the LORD has done this,
   the Holy One of Israel has created it.

Loss of Purpose

from Theology of Nature

So long as people were able to believe that they lived in a world that is purposively ordered (whether by a transcendent Creator or by some immanent principle), they were not troubled by the question of the purposiveness of their own lives. But when that belief was lost, as in ancient Gnosticism, or shaken, as it was by the Copernican revolution and subsequent scientific developments, the question of the purpose of human life was thrown into relief. Can meaning and purpose for human life be retrieved in a world from which they have vanished?

GEORGE S. HENDRY

Everyman

The weariness of life that has no will
To climb the steepening hill:
The sickness of the soul for sleep, and to be still
And then once more the impassioned pigmy fist
Clenched cloudward and defiant;
The pride that would prevail, the doomed protagonist
Grappling the ghostly giant.
Victim and venturer turn by turn, and then
Set free to be again
Companion in repose with those who once were men.

The mind of man environing its thought,
Wherein a world within this world is wrought, –
    A shadowed face alone in fields of light.
The lowly growth and long endeavour of will
That waits and watches from its human hill,
    A landmark tree looming against the night.

World undiscovered within us, radiant-white,
Through miracles of sight unmastered still,
Grant us the power to follow and to fulfil.

SIEGFRIED SASSOON (1886–1967)

Prayer for Rain

O God, make it rain!
Loose the sott silver passion of the rain!
Send swiftly from above
This clear token of Thy love.
Make it rain!

Deck the bushes and the trees
With the tassels of the rain.
Make the brooks pound to the seas
And the earth shine young again
God of passion, send the rain!

Oh, restore our ancient worth
With Thy rain!
Ease the heartache of the earth;
Sap the grain
Fill the valleys and the dales
With Thy silver slanting gales;
And through England and wild Wales
Send the rain!

Lord, restore us to Thy will
With the rain!
Soak the valley, drench the hill,
Drown the stain;
Smite the mountain's withered hips,
Wash the rouge from sunset's lips,
Fill the sky with singing ships.
Send the rain!

HERBERT PALMER (1880–1961)

The Face Behind the Veil

The Face Behind the Veil

The beauty of the world can remain unseen or appear faded unless the creator is recognised within his creation. I was talking recently to an elderly widow now living on her own in an isolated spot surrounded by garden and fields. The beauty of nature means a great deal to her. "But it is not everything," she said to me. "You have to know something else." We both knew she was talking of the Lord of Nature, though in everyday life and conversation it is often hard to find the right words. The heart of the truth in this case was recognised but unsaid.

The Piper at the Gates of Dawn

from The Wind in the Willows

On either side of them, as they glided onwards, the rich meadow-grass seemed that morning of a freshness and a greenness unsurpassable. Never had they noticed the roses so vivid, the willow-herb so riotous, the meadow-sweet so odorous and pervading. Then the murmur of the approaching weir began to hold the air, and they felt a consciousness that they were nearing the end, whatever it might be, that surely awaited their expedition.

A wide half-circle of foam and glinting lights and shining shoulders of green water, the great weir closed the backwater from bank to bank, troubled all the quiet surface with twirling eddies and floating foam-streaks, and deadened all other sounds with its solemn and soothing rumble. In midmost of the stream, embraced in the weir's shimmering arm-spread, a small island lay anchored, fringed close with willow and silver birch and alder. Reserved, shy, but full of significance, it hid whatever it might hold behind a veil, keeping it till the hour should come, and, with the hour, those who were called and chosen.

Slowly, but with no doubt or hesitation whatever, and in something of a solemn expectancy, the two animals passed through the broken, tumultuous water and moored their boat at the flowery margin of the island. In silence they landed, and pushed through the blossom and scented herbage and under-growth that led up to the level ground, till they stood on a little lawn of a marvellous green, set round with Nature's own orchard-trees – crab-apple, wild cherry, and slow.

"This is the place of my song-dream, the place the music played to me," whispered the Rat, as if in a trance. "Here, in this holy place, here if anywhere, surely we shall find Him!"

Then suddenly the Mole felt a great Awe fall upon him, an awe that turned his muscles to water, bowed his head, and rooted his feet to the ground.

KENNETH GRAHAME (1859–1932)

The Voice of Nature

There is a language wrote on earth and sky
By God's own pen in silent majesty;
There is a voice that's heard and felt and seen
In spring's young shades and summer's endless green;
There is a book of poesy and spells
In which that voice in sunny splendour dwells;
There is a page in which that voice aloud
Speaks music to the few and not the crowd;
Though no romantic scenes my feet have trod,
The voice of nature as the voice of God
Appeals to me in every tree and flower,
Breathing his glory, magnitude and power,
In nature's open book I read, and see
Beauty's rich lesson in this seeming-pea;
Crowds see no magic in the trifling thing;
Pshaw! 'tis a weed, and millions came with spring.
I hear rich music wheresoe'er I look,
But heedless worldlings chide the brawling brook;
And that small lark between me and the sky
Breathes sweetest strains of morning's melody;
Yet by the heedless crowd 'tis only heard
As the small warbling of a common bird
That o'er the plough teams hails the morning sun;
They see no music from such magic won.
Yet I see melody in nature's laws,
Or do I dream? – still wonder bids me pause:
I pause, and hear a voice that speaks aloud:
'Tis not on earth nor in the thundercloud;
The many look for sound – 'tis silence speaks,
And song like sunshine from her rapture breaks.
I hear it in my bosom ever near;
'Tis in these winds, and they are everywhere.
It casts around my vision magic spells
And makes earth heaven where poor fancy dwells.

I read its language, and its speech is joy;
So, without teaching when a lonely boy,
Each weed to me did happy tidings bring,
And laughing daisies wrote the name of spring,
And God's own language unto nature given
Seemed universal as the light of heaven
And common as the grass upon the plain,
That all may read and meet with joy again,
Save the unheeding heart that, like the tomb,
Shuts joy in darkness and forbids its bloom.

JOHN CLARE (1793–1864)

Nature's Spokesman

If I sometimes say that flowers smile
And if I happen to say
That rivers sing,
This does not mean I think there are smiles in flowers,

Songs in the running of rivers . . .
Such is my way to make false men aware
Of the truly real existence
Of rivers and flowers.

Since I write for them to read me, I sacrifice myself at times
To the stupidity of their feelings . . .
In this I do not agree
With myself: yet give myself
Absolution: I am that serious being
Nature's spokesman,
Since there are men who do not know
Nature's language –
Which is no language at all.

THOMAS MERTON (1915–1968)

The Veil of Nature

from Pray to Live

It is impressive to see how prayer opens one's eyes to nature. Prayer makes men contemplative and attentive. In place of manipulating, the man who prays stands receptive before the world. He no longer grabs but caresses, he no longer bites, but kisses, he no longer examines but admires. To this man, as for Merton, nature can show itself completely renewed. Instead of an obstacle, it becomes a way; instead of an invulnerable shield, it becomes a veil which gives a preview of unknown horizons.

HENRI J. M. NOUWEN (1932–)

Advent

from Morning, Noon and Night

Art Thou a stranger to my country, Lord?
My land of black roots and thick jungles
where the wild boar sharpens his tusks,
where the monkeys chatter in the trees,
and the peacock's shrill note
echoes through the mist-clad hills;
my land of brown, caked river mud
where the elephant and the leopard come to drink,
and the shambling bear with his dreamy eyes
sees the porcupine shedding his quills;
my land with its friezes of palmyra palms
etched sharply against the blue mountains;
my land of low-lying plains
with its miles of murmuring paddy fields
that stretch in undulating waves of green
to the distant horizon;
my land of sapphire skies and flaming sunsets,
my land of leaden grey skies piled high
with banks of monsoon clouds;
my land of stinging rain, of burning heat,
of dark nights, of enchanting moons
that dance behind the coconut fronds;
my land of tanks and pools
where the lazy buffalo wallows
and the red lotuses lie asleep?
Nay, Thou art no stranger, Lord,
for the wind whispers of Thee
and the waters chant Thy name.
The whole land is hushed in trembling expectancy,
awaiting Thy touch of creative Love.

CHANDRAN DEVANESEN

Light of the Sky

from St Joan

You think that life is nothing but not being stone dead. It is not the bread and water I fear: I can live on bread: when have I asked for more? It is no hardship to drink water if the water be clean. Bread has no sorrow for me, and water no affliction. But to shut me from the light of the sky and the sight of the fields and flowers; to chain my feet so that I can never again ride with the soldiers nor climb the hills; to make me breathe foul damp darkness, and keep from me everything that brings me back to the love of God when your wickedness and foolishness tempt me to hate Him: all this is worse than the furnace in the Bible that was heated seven times. I could do without my wardrobe; I could drag about in a skirt; I could let the banners and the trumpets and the knights and soldiers pass me and leave me behind as they leave the other women, if only I could still hear the wind in the trees, the larks in the sunshine, the young lambs crying through the healthy frost, and the blessed blessed church bells that send my angel voices floating to me on the wind . . . without those things I cannot live.

GEORGE BERNARD SHAW (1856–1950)

God Seen in Creation

Romans 1: 19–20

For what can be known about God is plain to them, because
God has shown it to them. Ever since the creation of the world
his invisible nature, namely, his eternal power and deity, has
been clearly perceived in the things that have been made.

God to know God

Acquaint thyself with God, if thou would'st taste
His works. Admitted once to his embrace,
Thou shalt perceive that thou was blind before:
Thine eye shall be instructed; and thine heart,
Made pure, shall relish, with divine delight
Till then unfelt, what hands divine have wrought.
Brutes graze the mountain-top, with faces prone
And eyes intent upon the scanty herb
It yields them; or, recumbent on its brow,
Ruminate heedless of the scene outspread
Beneath, beyond, and stretching far away
From inland regions to the distant main.
Man views it, and admires; but rests content
With what he views. The landscape has his praise,
But not its author. Unconcern'd who form'd
The paradise he sees, he finds it such,
And such well pleas'd to find it, asks no more.
Not so the mind that has been touch'd from heav'n,
And in the school of sacred wisdom taught
To read his wonders, in whose thought the world,
Fair as it is, existed ere it was.
Not for its own sake merely, but for his
Much more who fashion'd it, he gives it praise;
Praise that, from earth resulting, as it ought,
To earth's acknowledg'd sov'reign, finds at once
Its only just proprietor in Him.

WILLIAM COWPER (1731–1800)

Reality outside yourself

from Markings

A sunny day in March. Within the birch-tree's slender shadow on the crust of snow, the freezing stillness of the air is crystallised. Then – all of a sudden – the first blackbird's piercing note of call, a reality outside yourself, the real world. All of a sudden – the Earthly Paradise from which we have been excluded by our knowledge.

The devils enter uninvited when the house stands empty. For other kinds of guests, you have first to open the door.

DAG HAMMARSKJOLD (1905–1961)

Pure Religious Feeling

from Ethics

To have reverence in the face of life is to be in the grip of the eternal, unoriginated, forward-pushing will, which is the foundation of all being. It raises us above all intellectual knowledge of external objects, and grafts us on to the tree which is assured against drought because it is planted by the rivers of water. All vital religious feeling flows from reverence for life and for the necessity and for the need for ideals which is implicit in life. In reverence for life religious feeling lies before us in its most elemental and most profound form, in which it is no longer involved in explanations of the objective world, nor has anything to do with such, but is pure religious feeling founded altogether in implicit necessity and therefore devoid of care about results.

ALBERT SCHWEITZER (1875–1965)

The Gateway of the Spirit

Throughout my life, nature has provided me with a first stage refuge from the complexities of man and matter; with peace and space and reassurance. Unobtrusively, she has taught me more than all the books I've ever read, and led me naturally to meditation and the gateway of spirit. I have often been amazed at how isolated we can become from simple natural facts such as the cycles of life, the transitory and the eternal, the inexorability of natural law; and how easily, once taken away from nature, we get confused in our minds and lose touch with simple, basic common sense(s).

JOHN BUTLER (1939–)

Hymn to the Creator

O tell of his might, O sing of his grace,
whose robe is the light, whose canopy space;
his chariots of wrath the deep thunder clouds form,
and dark is his path on the wings of the storm.

The earth with its store of wonders untold,
almighty, thy power hath founded of old;
hath stablished it fast by a changeless decree,
and round it hath cast, like a mantle, the sea.

Thy bountiful care what tongue can recite?
it breathes in the air, it shines in the light;
it streams from the hills, it descends to the plain,
and sweetly distils in the dew and the rain.

ROBERT GRANT (1779–1838)

Nature and the God of Nature

from Scenes and Tales of Country Life

All Nature's works the curious mind employ,
Inspire a soothing melancholy joy;
Each rural sight, each sound, each smell, combine;
The tinkling sheep bell, or the breath of kine;
The new-mown hay that scents the swelling breeze,
Or cottage-chimney smoking through the trees.

REV. GILBERT WHITE

We are all of us apt to speak of Nature as distinct from the Great Creator of heaven and earth. Dr Donne says, "Nature was God's apprentice, to learn in the first seven days, and now is his foreman, and works next under him." Few will venture to deny this. Every thing we see around us affords proofs of divine workmanship and divine arrangement. "Survey the heavens, the work of His fingers, the moon and the stars which he had ordained"; consider the boundless extent, the immeasurable height of the vault above us; see the sun rising in the east, succeeded by the moon in all her pensive beauty – look at the earth, clothed with verdure, and rich with its variety of produce, and we shall be obliged to acknowledge that nothing has come from the hand of the Divine Creator, but what is excellent and perfect in its kind, adapted with infinite skill to its proper place, and fitted for its intended use. Happy are they who give themselves to the contemplation of these works, and find pleasure and improvement in the study of them.

EDWARD JESSE

Ancient Religion

from English Downland

The antiquary, Leland, called the barrows congregated in the neighbourhood of Stonehenge, *monticuli*, and little downs they are, set upon the shoulders of the greater. The religious ideas of the ancients, fantastic as we may think them, voiced this union of Man with Nature. It is obvious that the men of 2000 B.C. and onwards preferred the chalk, partly because it gave them abundance of flint for tilth and homestead and sepulchte, and partly because the hills were open land, lifted above the watery and tree-tenebrous wastes of the valleys. But they also brought with them a sense of the holiness of the high place as a stepping-stone to the sky-world. The burial tump was the house of the dead reborn and with the stone circle, also sepulchral in origin, a kind of emblem of eternity, or at least of life that travelled through death and on and on like the ridges of the chalk into the western sky. Archaic rites of fertility and resurrection were hardly science-proof. But they were concerned with the elementals of life and death and their monuments are appropriate to the curves and sweeps of the bare down that shake off the confinement of the vale. Barrow and height on which it stands symbolise alike the marriage of heaven and earth.

H. J. MASSINGHAM (1888–1952)

The Glory of God

Psalm 19: 1–6

The heavens declare the glory of God: and the firmament sheweth his handy-work.

One day telleth another: and one night certifieth another.

There is neither speech nor language: but their voices are heard among them.

Their sound is gone out into all lands: and their words into the ends of the world.

In them hath he set a tabernacle for the sun: which cometh forth as a bridegroom out of his chamber, and rejoiceth as a giant to run his course.

It goeth forth from the uttermost part of the heaven, and runneth about unto the end of it again: and there is nothing hid from the heat thereof.

How Great Thou Art

O Lord, my God,
    when I in awesome wonder,
consider all the worlds
    thy hand has made,
I see the stars,
    I hear the rolling thunder,
thy power throughout
    the universe displayed.

Then sings my soul,
    my Saviour God, to thee:
How great thou art,
    how great thou art.

When through the woods
    and forest glades I wander
and hear the birds
    sing sweetly in the trees:
when I look down
    from loftly mountain grandeur,
and hear the brook,
    and feel the gentle breeze:

Then sings my soul,
    my Saviour God, to thee:
How great thou art,
    how great thou art.

STUART K. HINE

Be as the Air

That God is present in all places, that he sees every action, hears all discourses, and understands every thought, is no strange thing to a Christian ear, who hath been taught his doctrine not only by right reason and the consent of all the wise men in the world, but also by God Himself in Holy Scripture. "Am I a God at hand, saith the Lord, and not a God far off." Can any hide himself in secret places, that I shall not see him? said the Lord; do not I fill heaven and earth? "Neither is there any creature that is not manifest in His sight; but all things are naked and open before the eyes of Him with whom we have to do." "In Him we live and move and have our being." God is wholly in every place, included in no place; not bound with bands except those of love; not divided into parts, not changeable into several shapes; filling heaven and earth with His present power and with His never absent nature. So that we may imagine God and be as the air and the sea, and we are all enclosed in this circle, wrapped up in the lap of this infinite nature, or as infants in the wombs of their pregnant mothers; and we can no more be removed from the presence of God than from our own being.

JEREMY TAYLOR (1613–1667)

Hurrahing in Harvest

Summer ends now; now, barbarous in beauty, the stooks rise
   Around; up above, what wind-walks! what lovely behaviour
   Of silk-sack clouds! has wilder, wilful-wavier
Meal-drift moulded ever and melted across skies?

I walk, I lift up, I lift up heart, eyes,
   Down all that glory in the heavens to glean our Saviour;
   And, eyes, heart, what looks, what lips yet gave you a
Rapturous love's greeting of realer, of rounder replies?

And the azurous hung hills are his world-wielding shoulder
   Majestic – as a stallion stalwart, very-violet-sweet! –
These things, these things were here and but the beholder
   Wanting; which two when they once meet,
The heart rears wings bold and bolder
   And hurls for him, O half hurls each for him off under his
     feet.

GERARD MANLEY HOPKINS (1844–1889)

God's Grandeur

The world is charged with the grandeur of God.
  It will flame out, like shining from shook foil;
  It gathers to a greatness, like the ooze of oil
Crushed. Why do men then now not reck his rod?
Generations have trod, have trod, have trod;
  And all is seared with trade; bleared, smeared with toil;
  And wears man's smudge and shares man's smell: the soil
Is bare now, nor can foot feel, being shod.

And for all this, nature is never spent;
  There lives the dearest freshness deep down things;
And though the last lights off the black West went
  Oh, morning, at the brown brink eastward, springs –
Because the Holy Ghost over the bent
  World broods with warm breast and with ah! bright wings.

GERARD MANLEY HOPKINS (1844–1889)

What is my God?

from Confessions

But what do I love when I love my God? Not material beauty or beauty of a temporal order; not the brilliance of earthly light, so welcome to our eyes; not the sweet melody of harmony and song; not the fragrance of flowers, perfumes, and spices; not manna or honey; not limbs such as the body delights to embrace. It is not these that I love when I love my God. And yet, when I love him, it is true that I love a light of a certain kind, a voice, a perfume, a food, an embrace; but they are of the kind that I love in my inner self, when my soul is bathed in light that is not bound by space; when it listens to sound that never dies away; when it breathes fragrance that is not borne away on the wind; when it tastes food that is never consumed by the eating; when it clings to an embrace from which it is not severed by fulfilment of desire. This is what I love when I love my God.

But what is my God? I put my question to the earth. It answered, "I am not God," and all things on earth declared the same. I asked the sea and the chasms of the deep and the living things that creep in them, but they answered, "We are not your God. Seek what is above us." I spoke to the winds that blow, and the whole air and all that lives in it replied, "Anaximenes is wrong. I am not God." I asked the sky, the sun, the moon, and the stars, but they told me, 'Neither are we the God whom you seek." I spoke to all the things that are about me, all that can be admitted by the door of the senses, and I said, "Since you are not my God, tell me about him. Tell me something of my God." Clear and loud then answered, "God is he who made us." I asked these questions simply by gazing at these things, and their beauty was all the answer they gave.

SAINT AUGUSTINE OF HIPPO (354–430)

The Meaning of the Word Beautiful

from Modern Painters

I was lying by this fountain – on a dark evening of July, dark not with night, but with storm. The precipice above me lost itself in the air within fifty feet of my head – not in cloud – but in the dark, motionless atmosphere. The lower boughs of its pines shook like black plumes against the shade; their pointed tops faded into its body – faint as if woven of gossamer – spectral shadows of colossal strength. The valley lay for leagues on either side – roofed with the impenetrable gloom – walled with the steep bases of its hill – one boundless chamber – lighted only as it seemed, by the white foam of the forked Arve – cast like a stream of lightning along its floor. Through the veil of cloud, the presence of the great mountains was indicated only by the sound of their forests, by the sharp, sudden stroke – like a human cry, – the wail of the glacier upon its path of pain, and the gust – rising by fits and falling – of the wind, or the waves, the ear knew not which – among their chasms.

So it had been through the day – no rain – no motion – no light. One roof – one level veil, as of God's Holy Place, and the voices of the mountains from behind it and above.

I lay beside the fountain – watching the motion of its soundless domes, and the entangling within its depth of the green blades with their own shadows. From the rock above, a single oozy drop fell at intervals into the pool, with a sound like that of a passing bell far away. Among the thick herbage at its edge the grasshoppers, heavy and faint in the chill and darkness, climbed freely up the jointed stalks, staring about them with their black beaded eyes, and fell, rustling, – unable to lift their scarlet wings. It was as if the sun had been taken away from the world, and the life of the earth were ebbing away, groan by groan.

Suddenly, there came in the direction of Dome du Goûter a crash – of prolonged thunder; and when I looked up, I saw the cloud cloven, as it were by the avalanche itself, whose white stream came bounding down the eastern slope of the mountain, like slow lightning. The vapour parted before its fall, pierced by the whirlwind of its motion; the gap widened, the dark shade melted away on either side; and, like a risen spirit casting off its garment of corruption, and flushed with eternity of life, the Aiguilles of the south broke through the black foam of the storm clouds. One by one, pyramid above pyramid, the mighty range of its companions shot off their shrouds, and took to themselves their glory – all fire – no shade – no dimness. Spire of ice – dome of snow – wedge of rock – *all* fire in the light of the sunset, sank into the hollows of the crags – and pierced through the prisms of the glaciers, and dwelt within them – as it does in clouds. The ponderous storm writhed and moaned beneath them, the forests wailed and waved in the evening wind, the steep river flashed and leaped along the valley; but the mighty pyramids stood calmly – in the very heart of the high heaven – a celestial city with walls of amethyst and gates of gold – filled with the light and clothed with the Peace of God. And then I learned – what till then I had not known – the real meaning of the word Beautiful. With all that I had ever seen before – there had come mingled the associations of humanity – the exertion of human power – the action of human mind. The image of self had not been effaced in that of God. It was then only beneath those glorious hills that I learned how thought itself may become ignoble and energy itself become base – when compared with the absorption of soul and spirit – the prostration of all power – and the cessation of all will – before, and in the Presence of, the manifested Deity. It was then only that I understood that to become nothing might be to become more than Man; – how without desire – without memory – without sense even of existence – the very sense of its own lost perception of a mightier – the immortal soul might

71

be held for ever – impotent as a leaf – yet greater than tongue can tell – wrapt in the one contemplation of the Infinite God.

JOHN RUSKIN (1819–1900)

God is real

"What a happiness, what a joy it is to be *quite* sure that there is a God, not anything built up by mere human reasoning, no clever or subtle hypothesis, nothing particularly French or German or English, but something as infinitely more real than the air around us, and the pollen of the flowers, and the flight of the birds, and the trials and troubles and the needs of our little lives stimulated and enriched by the lives of creatures so different from ourselves, touching us continually all round; and the fundamental assurance is not simply one of variety or even of richness, it is an assurance accompanying and crowning all such variety, of a reality, of the Reality, one and harmonious, strong and self-sufficing, of God."

BARON FRIEDRICH VON HUGEL (1852–1925)

The Leaping Saga of Prayer

Night and the reindeer on the clouds above the haycocks
And the wings of the great roc ribboned for the fair!
The leaping saga of prayer! And high, there, on the hare-
                        Heeled winds the rooks
Cawing from their black bethels soaring, the holy books
Of birds! Among the cocks like fire the red fox

Burning! Night and the vein of birds in the winged, sloe wrist
Of the wood! Pastoral beat of blood through the laced leaves!

The stream from the priest black wristed spinney and sleeves
                        Of thistling frost
Of the nightingale's din and tale! The upgiven ghost
Of the dingle torn to singing and the surpliced

Hill of cypresses! The din and tale in the skimmed
Yard of the buttermilk rain on the pail! The sermon
Of blood! The bird loud vein! The saga from mermen
                        To seraphim
Leaping! The gospel rooks! All tell, this night, of him
Who comes as red as the fox and sly as the heeled wind.

Illumination of music! the lulled black-backed
Gull, on the wave with sand in its eyes! And the foal moves
Through the shaken greensward lake, silent, on moonshod
   hooves,
                        In the winds' wakes.
Music of elements, that a miracle makes!
Earth, air, water, fire, singing into the white act,

The haygold haired, my love asleep, and the rift blue
Eyed, in the haloed house, in her rareness and hilly
High riding, held and blessed and true, and so stilly
                        Lying the sky

Might cross its planets, the bell weep, night gather her eyes,
The Thief fall on the dead like the willy nilly dew,

Only for the turning of the earth in her holy
Heart! Slyly, slowly, hearing the wound in her side go
Round the sun, he comes to my love like the designed snow,
                    And truly he
Flows to the strand of flowers like the dew's ruly sea,
And surely he sails like the ship shape clouds. Oh he
Comes designed to my love to steal not her tide raking
Wound, nor her riding high, nor her eyes, nor kindled hair,
But her faith that each vast night and the saga of prayer
                        He comes to take
Her faith that this last night for his unsacred sake
He comes to leave her in the lawless sun awaking

Naked and forsaken to grieve he will not come.
Ever and ever by all your vows believe and fear
My dear this night he comes and night without end my dear
                    Since you were born:
And you shall wake, from country sleep, this dawn and each
    first dawn,
Your faith as deathless as the outcry of the ruled sun.

DYLAN THOMAS (1914–1953)

Love's Dance

from Orchestra

Dancing, bright lady, then began to be,
   When the first seeds whereof the world did spring,
The fire, air, earth, and water, did agree
   By Love's persuasion, nature's mighty king,
   To leave their first discorded combating,
     And in a dance such measure to observe,
     As all the world their motion should preserve.

Since when they still are carried in a round,
   And changing come one in another's place;
Yet do they neither mingle nor confound,
   But every one doth keep the bounded space
   Wherein the dance doth bid it turn or trace.
     This wondrous miracle did Love devise,
     For dancing is love's proper exercise.

Like this he framed the gods' eternal bower,
   And of a shapeless and confused mass,
By his through-piercing and digesting power,
   The turning vault of heaven formed was,
   Whose starry wheels he hath so made to pass,
     As that their movings do a music frame,
     And they themselves still dance unto the same.

Or if this all, which round about we see,
   As idle Morpheus some sick brains hath taught,
Of undivided motes compacted be,
   How was this goodly architecture wrought?
   Or by what means were they together brought?

They err that say they did concur by chance;
Love made them meet in a well-ordered dance!

SIR JOHN DAVIES (1569–1626)

The Stupendous Whole

from An Essay on Man

See, thro' this air, this ocean, and this earth,
All matter quick, and bursting into birth.
Above, how high, progressive life may go!
Around, how wide! how deep extend below!
Vast chain of Being, which from God began,
Natures aethereal, human, angel, man,
Beast, bird, fish, insect! what no eye can see,
No glass can reach! from Infinite to thee,
From thee to Nothing! – On superior pow'rs
Were we to press, inferior might on ours:
Or in the full creation leave a void,
Where, one step broken, the great scale's destroy'd:
From Nature's chain whatever link you strike,
Tenth or ten thousandth, breaks the chain alike.
And if each system in gradation roll,
Alike essential to th'amazing whole;
The least confusion but in one, not all
That system only, but the whole must fall.
Let Earth unbalanc'd from her orbit fly,
Planets and Suns run lawless thro' the sky,
Let ruling Angels from their spheres he hurl'd,
Being on being wreck'd, and world on world,
Heav'n's whole foundations to their centre nod,
And nature tremble to the throne of God:
All this dread ORDER break – for whom? For thee?
Vile worm! – oh Madness, Pride, Impiety!

All are but parts of one stupendous whole,
Whose body Nature is, and God the soul;
That, chang'd thro' all, and yet in all the same,
Great in the earth, as in th'aethereal frame,
Warms in the sun, refreshes in the breeze,

Glows in the stars, and blossoms in the trees,
Lives thro' all life, extends thro' all extent,
Spreads undivided, operates unspent,
Breathes in our soul, informs our mortal part,
As full, as perfect, in a hair as heart;
As full, as perfect, in vile Man that mourns,
As the rapt Seraph that adores and burns;
To him no high, no low, no great, no small;
He fills, he bounds, connects, and equals all.

ALEXANDER POPE (1688–1744)

Seasons,

Associations and Spirit

Seasons, Associations and Spirit

Someone, aware of what people lack when they live cocooned urban lives, recommended growing lettuce seed in a bowl. Watching the plantlets develop is an activity somehow conducive to health and wholeness. In a miniscule way the grower becomes aware of the conditions of growth which are good for him as well as the lettuce. To the town dweller all times of year may be the same and peas eaten for lunch every Sunday. Not so for the country gardener.

The natural world should play an essential part in our daily lives and in our spiritual awareness. In this section I have directed attention not so much to the familiar scientific descriptions of the balance and harmony of nature but to the inward and spiritual independency which also undergird the practical and physical.

The Influence of Spring

from The Prologue to The Canterbury Tales

Whan that Aprille with his shoures sote
The droghte of Marche hath perced to the rote,
And bathed every veyne in swich licour,
Of which vertu engendred is the flour;
Whan Zephirus eek with his swete breeth
Inspired hath in every holt and heeth
The tendre croppes, and the yonge sonne
Hath in the Ram his halfe cours y-ronne,
And smale fowles maken melodye,
That slepen al the night with open yë,
(So priketh hem nature in hir corages):
Than longen folk to goon on pilgrimages
(And palmers for to seken straunge strondes)
To ferne halwes, couthe in sondry londes;
And specially, from every shires ende
Of Engelond, to Caunterbury they wende,
The holy blisful martir for to seke,
That hem hath holpen, whan that they were seke.
Bifel that, in that seson on a day,
In Southwerk at the Tabard as I lay
Redy to wenden on my pilgrimage
To Caunterbury with ful devout corage,
At night was come in-to that hostelrye
Wel nyne and twenty in a companye,
Of sondry folk, by aventure y-falle
In felawships, and pilgrims were they alle,
That toward Caunterbury wolden ryde;

GEOFFREY CHAUCER (?1340–1400)

84

The Influence of Natural Objects

Wisdom and Spirit of the universe!
Thou Soul, that art the Eternity of thought!
And giv'st to forms and images a breath
And everlasting motion! not in vain,
By day or star-light, thus from my first dawn
Of childhood didst thou intertwine for me
The passions that build up our human soul;
Not with the mean and vulgar works of Man;
But with high objects, with enduring things,
With life and nature; purifying thus
The elements of feeling and of thought,
And sanctifying by such discipline
Both pain and fear, – until we recognise
A grandeur in the beatings of the heart.

Nor was this fellowship vouchsafed to me
With stinted kindness. In November days,
When vapours rolling down the valleys made
A lonely scene more lonesome; among woods
At noon; and 'mid the calm of summer nights,
When, by the margin of the trembling lake,
Beneath the gloomy hills, homeward I went
In solitude, such intercourse was mine:
Mine was it in the fields both day and night,
And by the waters, all the summer long.
And in the frosty season, when the sun
Was set, and, visible for many a mile,
The cottage-windows through the twilight blazed.
I heeded not the summons: happy time
It was indeed for all of us; for me
It was a time of rapture! Clear and loud
The village-clock tolled six – I wheeled about,
Proud and exulting like an untired horse
That cares not for his home. – All shod with steel

We hissed along the polished ice, in games
Confederate, imitative of the chase
And woodland pleasures, – the resounding horn,
The pack loud-chiming, and the hunted hare.
So through the darkness and the cold we flew,
And not a voice was idle: with the din
Smitten, the precipices rang aloud;
The leafless trees and every icy crag
Tinkled like iron; while far-distant hills
Into the tumult sent an alien sound
Of Melancholy not unnoticed, while the stars,
Eastward, were sparkling clear, and in the west
The orange sky of evening died away.

Not seldom from the uproar I retired
Into a silent bay, or sportively
Glanced sideway, leaving the tumultuous throng,
To cut across the reflex of a star;

. . . and I stood and watched
Till all was tranquil as a summer sea.

WILLIAM WORDSWORTH (1770–1850)

Green Living

from The Green Guide

For nearly fifteen years now – and after a quarter of a century of the infernal tumult of life in Paris – I have been living in a mill house deep in a green valley in Auvergne where, apart from a few passing planes, the only sounds to be heard are the sounds invented by nature: the birdsong which varies with the seasons, the chirping of the crickets in summer, the rustling of the spring breeze and the roar of the winter wind in the alders and the poplar trees, the cool ripple of the river by the walls of the house or its angry boom when the waters are in full spate.

Here I have learned that the key to happiness lies in a return to those simple truths which were born with our distant ancestors and confirmed by centuries of experience. Wisdom and common sense are one and the same thing; we are wrong to forget the fact or to obscure it with pretentious intellectual edifices that are part of the great myth of progress at all costs. Technology, however advanced, cannot solve everything, and it is not by a routine investigation of the cosmos that man will achieve a sense of peace.

By having less ambitious aims, by turning once more to the age-old customs and traditions from which, willingly or unwillingly, he has allowed himself to depart, he would again be in touch with a world that fits him – a world of which the "environment", on which too much ink and breath is being spent today, is part; he would return to his true nature, becoming free of most of those artificial problems that burden him on all sides; once this essential balance was restored, he could become aware of his rightful place in the universe and all that it had to offer; he would conform to the rules which order his well-being and hence experience a genuine joie de vivre.

Since man first began to reflect on his nature and record his conclusions in writing, many have voiced the opinion that happiness – a goal to which all aspire – resides in a few simple rules. Essentially, all we have to do is to obey nature, the reflection of the wisdom of creation (and therefore of the Creator).

The rule is that the more delicate and beautiful the flower and fruit the closer must be the union with earth. And the point of contact is the root. There colour and scent are made; there the hundred-foot tree lies in little; there the petal that a dewdrop almost destroys is held safe under the ponderous earth. In the root, when April comes, Someone awakes, rubs drowsy eyes, stretches drowsy hands, remembers a dream of light that troubled its sleep, and begins, with infinite precautions, finesse and courage, to work the miracle of which it has knowledge; "eagerly watching for its flower and fruit, anxious its little soul looks out."

Surely no idea of God could so well hint of Him as this idea of the root – of the great root of a forest tree, hawsered in the heart of matter; upholding matter; transforming matter by a secret alchemy into beauty that goes out from mystery – lives its day – returns, weary, into mystery, and is again renewed. "None can tell how from so small a centre come such sweets."

JEAN PALAISANT

The Pine and the National Character

from Modern Painters

I have watched them in such scenes with the deeper interest, because of all trees they have hitherto had most influence on human character. The effect of other vegetation, however great, has been divided by mingled species; elm and oak in England, poplar in France, birch in Scotland, olive in Italy and Spain, share their power with inferior trees, and with all the changing charm of successive agriculture. But the tremendous unity of the pine absorbs and moulds the life of a race. The pine shadows rest upon a nation. The Northern peoples, century after century, lived under one or other of the two great powers of the Pine and the Sea, both infinite. They dwelt amidst the forests, as they wandered on the waves and saw no end, nor any other horizon, still the dark green trees, or the dark green waters, jagged the dawn with their fringe or their foam. And whatever elements of imagination, or of warrior strength, or of domestic justice, were brought down by the Norwegian and the Goth against the dissoluteness or degradation of the South of Europe, were taught them under the green roofs and wild penetralia of the pine.

JOHN RUSKIN (1819–1900)

Evolution

from Paracelsus

The centre-fire heaves underneath the earth,
And the earth changes like a human face;
The molten ore bursts up among the rocks,
Winds into the stone's heart, outbranches bright
In hidden mines, spots barren river-beds,
Crumbles into fine sand where sunbeams bask –
God joys therein. The wroth sea's waves are edged
With foam, white as the bitten lip of hate,
When, in the solitary waste, strange groups
Of young volcanos come up, cyclops-like,
Staring together with their eyes on flame –
God tastes a pleasure in their uncouth pride.
Then all it still; earth is a wintry clod:
But spring-wind, like a dancing psaltress, passes
Over its breast to waken it, rare verdure
Buds tenderly upon rough banks, between
The withered tree-roots and the cracks of frost,
Like a smile striving with a wrinkled face;
The grass grows bright, the boughs are swoln with blooms
Like chrysalids impatient for the air,
The shining dorrs are busy, beetles run
Along the furrows, ants make their ado;
Above, birds fly in merry flocks, the lark
Soars up and up, shivering for very joy;
Afar the ocean sleeps; white fishing-gulls
Flit where the strand is purple with its tribe
Of nested limpets; savage creatures seek
Their loves in wood and plain – and God renews
His ancient rapture. Thus he dwells in all,
From life's minute beginnings, up at last
To man – the consummation of this scheme
Of being, the completion of this sphere

Of life: whose attributes had here and there
Been scattered o'er the visible world before,
Asking to be combined, dim fragments meant
To be united in some wondrous whole,
Imperfect qualities throughout creation,
Suggesting some one creature yet to make,
Some point where all those scattered rays should meet
Convergent in the faculties of man . . .
Hints and previsions of which faculties
Are strewn confusedly everywhere about
The inferior natures, and all lead up higher,
All shape out dimly the superior race,
The heir of hopes too fair to turn out false,
And man appears at last.

ROBERT BROWNING (1812–1889)

Praise the Lord

Psalm 104: 1–24

Praise the Lord, O my soul; O Lord my soul: thou art become exceeding glorious; thou art clothed with majesty and honour.

Thou deckest thyself with light as it were with a garment: and spreadest out the heavens like a curtain.

Who layeth the beams of his chambers in the waters: and maketh the clouds his chariot, and walketh upon the wings of the wind.

He maketh his angels spirits: and his ministers a flaming fire.

He laid the foundations of the earth: that it never should move at any time.

Thou coveredst it with the deep like as with a garment: the waters stand in the hills.

At thy rebuke they flee: at the voice of thy thunder they are afraid.

They go up as high as the hills, and down to the valleys beneath: even unto the place which thou hast appointed for them.

Thou hast set them their bounds which they shall not pass: neither turn again to cover the earth.

He sendeth the springs into the rivers: which run among the hills.

All beasts of the field drink thereof: and the wild asses quench their thirst.

Beside them shall the fowls of the air have their habitation: and sing among the branches.

He watereth the hills from above: the earth is filled with the fruit of thy works.

He bringeth forth grass for the cattle: and green herb for the service of men;

That he may bring food out of the earth, and wine that maketh glad the heart of man: and oil to make him a cheerful countenance, and bread to strengthen man's heart.

The trees of the Lord also are full of sap: even the cedars of Libanus which he hath planted;

Wherein the birds make their nests: and the fir-trees are a dwelling for the stork.

The high hills are a refuge for the wild goats and so are the stony rocks for the conies.

He appointed the moon for certain seasons and the sun knoweth his going down.

Thou makest darkness that it may be night wherein all the beasts of the forest do move.

The lions roaring after their prey: do seek their meat from God.

The sun ariseth, and they get them away together: and lay them down in their dens.

Man goeth forth to his work, and to his labour until the evening.

O Lord, how manifold are thy works: in wisdom hast thou made them all; the earth is full of thy riches.

If love walks with you

If you have a thousand reasons for living,
If you never feel alone,
if you wake up wanting to sing,
if everything speaks to you,
from the stone in the road
to the star in the sky,
from the loitering lizard
to the fish, lord of the sea,
if you understand the winds
and listen to the silence,
rejoice,
for love walks with you,
he is your comrade,
is your brother!

HELDER CAMARA (1909)

His Damascus Road

from Old Rectory

OLD RECTORY
It was possession in a different sense –
I was possessed by it. For, suburb-bred,
I had a pavement boyhood. Larks for me
Were pranks, not birds. The apple-blossom's tinge
I never noticed; nor the change of sky
(The hoarding's change I did) except when clouds
Threatened a game of tennis, later golf.
(How far those pastimes make past times recede;
Remote as stoolball seems a stymie now).
My walks were shopwards, past the numbered gates
Or parlour-like front-gardens, privet-walled,
Down to the Broadway's fascia-fascination.
Summer meant longer days, and little else;
And when day switched to night, the evening star
Had no clear call for me; such things I missed,
And even puberty did not assist.
And when in manhood I became aware,
Belatedly and fervently aware
Of nature's loveliness, it was as if
I saw with the same eyes, but different sight,
Myself the convert, a converted world.
For if small things may be compared with great,
A country lane was my Damascus Road.

FOSSICK
And it was this experience, no doubt,
That prompted your self-exile.

OLD RECTORY   Exile? No,
Say rather my escape from exile, from
Confinement in the Siburberia

95

Of streets, its climate harsh with tarmac Junes
And privet Aprils. How it irked my spirit
To see a frost that whitened absent woods
Squander its scintillating treasury
On breakfast terraces; or misty shafts
Of soft October moonlight mock themselves
In lamp-post glades; or beautifying snow
Reverse its mask, and make a dreary street
More dreary, shovelled into grimey mumps.
I took to flight.

    BAYTRE   And, as you have described,
Found your first cottage on a village fringe.

    OLD RECTORY
And even there my cell would have become
As irksome as a prison's on fine days,
Had I been window-bound. No boon to me
To watch the autumn sunlight slowly shelve
Its vapour, if I watched it from a room.
I longed to be abroad and on the bank
Of gorse which spider-myriads had draped
In jewelled mist, unconsciously creating
Infinite riches with their little looms.
A rainbow always fetched me out of doors,
As if its spectrum were a spectacle
Too wide for windows, which I had to stand
And stare at in the open, and stare on
Until it dwindled to a coloured stub
Tingeing a tower. So, too, a likely cloud,
Serry or scud, would hurry me uphill
To watch its windy muster in the sky.
So, too, like times of festival for me
Were snow and mist and flood – for if I loved
The landscape as it was from day to day,
How much more, when they were enhancing it
With wooded whiteness or swathed distances

96

Or fields that ferried a reflected swan.
All day was then a walk: trudge, pause and stare,
An eager strider up each hill, and on
Its brow an eager statue; and, perhaps,
When home I'd plodded, just at candle time
And taken to my fireside, the glimpsed moon
Rising, would fetch me out to gaze again,
Entranced and rivetted, until my viewing
Became a kind of vigil, and I longed
For some quick cloud to edge across the night
And moon go in, so I could go in too.

MARTYN SKINNER (1906–)

Beneath the Crust

from Mysticism

Yet the course of this transcendence, this amazing inward journey, was closely linked, first and last, with the processes of human life. It sprang from that life, as man springs from the sod. We were even able to describe it under those symbolic formulae which we are accustomed to call the "laws" of the natural world. By an extension of these formulae, their logical application, we discovered a path which led us without a break from the sensible to the supra-sensible; from apparent to absolute life. There is nothing unnatural about the Absolute of the mystics: He sets the rhythm of His own universe, and confirms to the harmonies which He had made. We, deliberately seeking for that which we suppose to be spiritual, too often overlook that which alone is Real. The true mysteries of life accomplish themselves so softly, with so easy and assured a grace, so frank an acceptance of our breeding, striving, dying, and unresting world, that the unimaginative natural man – all agog for the marvellous – is hardly startled by their daily and radiant revelation of infinite wisdom and love. Yet this revelation presses incessantly upon us. Only the hard crust of surface-consciousness conceals it from our normal sight. In some least expected moment, the common activities of life in progress, that Reality in Whom the mystics dwell slips through our closed doors, and suddenly we see It at our side.

EVELYN UNDERHILL (1875–1941)

Light Restored

from Ode on Intimations of Immortality

O joy! that in our embers
Is something that doth live,
That nature yet remembers
What was so fugitive!
The thought of our past years in me doth breed
Perpetual benediction: not indeed
For that which is most worthy to be blest;
Delight and liberty, the simple creed
Of Childhood, whether busy or at rest,
With new-fledged hope still fluttering in his breast: –
    Not for these I raise
    The song of thanks and praise;
    But for those obstinate questionings
    Of sense and outward things,
    Fallings from us, vanishings;
    Blank misgivings of a Creature
Moving about in worlds not realised,
High instincts before which our mortal Nature
Did tremble like a guilty Thing surprised:
    But for those first affections,
    Those shadowy recollections,
    Which, be they what they may,
Are yet the fountain-light of all our day,
Are yet a master-light of all our seeing;
    Uphold us, cherish, and have power to make
Our noisy years seem moments in the being
Of the eternal Silence: truths that wake,
    To perish never:
Which neither listlessness, nor mad endeavour,
    Nor Man nor Boy,
Nor all that is at enmity with joy,
Can utterly abolish or destroy!

Hence in a season of calm weather
Though inland far we be,
Our Souls have sight of that immortal sea
Which brought us hither,
Can in a moment travel thither,
And see the Children sport upon the shore,
And hear the mighty waters rolling evermore.

WILLIAM WORDSWORTH (1770–1850)

Wind Wave and Spirit

from Afoot in England

But, no, there was one more, marvellous as any – the experience of a day of days, one of those rare days when nature appears to us spiritualised and is no longer nature, when that which had transfigured this visible world is in us too, and it becomes possible to believe – it is almost a conviction – that the burning and shining spirit seen and recognised in one among a thousand we have known is in all of us and in all things. In such moments it is possible to go beyond even the most advanced of the modern physicists who holds that force alone exists, that matter is but a disguise, a shadow and delusion; for we may add that force itself – that which we call force or energy – is but a semblance and shadow of the universal soul.

W. H. HUDSON (1841–1922)

Affinity with the Animal

from St Hugh of Lincoln

Yet another element in his life which attracts many is his
special affinity to the animal creation. When he was a monk
at the Grande Chartreuse, he became attached to a small bird
called a burnet which he tamed until his prior forbade him.
Birds and squirrels at Witham also seemed attracted to his
company. But the most famous example of this affinity is the
swan in his manor at Stow. Accounts by Adam and by Gerald
of Wales are eye-witness accounts, but some of the details have
puzzled naturalists of our own day. This swan became both pet
and watchdog. Near the end of Hugh's life, the swan's strange
behaviour was regarded as a symbol of the saint's attitude to
death, anticipated with joy rather than fear. However this may
be, Gerald's description is full of interest:

A swan suddenly arrived which had never been seen there
before. In a few days it had fought all the other swans there;
being larger and heavier than them, it killed them all except
one female. It was about as much larger than a swan as a
swan is larger than a goose; but in everything else, especially
its white colour, it closely resembled a swan except that it
was not only larger but also did not have the usual swelling
and black streak on its beak. Instead, that part of its beak
was flat and bright yellow in colour, as also were its head
and the upper part of its neck.

This royal bird of unusual appearance and size suddenly
became completely tame when the bishop arrived at this
place. It let itself be captured without difficulty and was
brought to the bishop for him to admire . . . When he fed
it, the bird used to thrust its long neck up his wide and ample
sleeve so that its head lay on his breast; for a little while it
would remain there, hissing gently, as if it were talking

fondly and happily to its master and asking something from him . . .

Whenever the bishop returned after one of his usual absences, for three or four days before the swan displayed more excitement than usual. It flew over the surface of the river, beating the water with its wings and giving vent to loud cries. From time to time it left the pond and hastily strode either to the hall or the gate as if going to meet its master on his arrival . . .

Curiously enough, it was friendly and tame to nobody except the bishop; as I have seen myself, it kept everyone else away from its master when it was with him by hissing at them and threatening them with wings and beak, emitting loud croaks as is the habit of swans. It seemed determined to make it quite clear that it belonged only to him and was a symbol sent to the bishop alone.

It would allow no man, no dog nor any other animal to walk beside the bishop or go near him; it frequently attacked the bishop's chaplain and biographer. The keepers of the manor would know that the bishop was coming soon when they heard the swan's unusual cries. But when Hugh visited Stow at Easter 1200 it would not come to meet him. When it was captured at last, its hanging head and general air of wretchedness made it the very picture of grief. Afterwards people realized that it was taking leave of its master for the last time. However it survived him for many years.

D. H. FARMER

Nature mystic

from Saint Francis: Nature Mystic

Saint Francis was not only a mystic but a nature mystic. Like Clement of Alexandria before him, he saw nature as sanctified by the Incarnation; and like William Blake later, he could see heaven in a wild flower. The evidence does not depend on the stories of his tender dealings with animals, though these may be cited in support. Celano tells us:

> When he considered the glory of the flowers, how happy he was to gaze at the beauty of their forms and to enjoy their marvellous fragrance! How easily his spirit would take wing and rise to meditating on the beauty of that unique flower that blossomed fair as the approaching spring, from "the root of Jesse" and by its fragrance brought new life to countless men who were dead in their souls!
>
> When he found many flowers growing together, it might happen that he would speak to them and encourage them, as though they could understand, to praise the Lord. It was the same with the fields of corn and the vineyards, the stones in the earth and in the woods, all the beauteous meadows, the tinkling brooks, the sprouting gardens, earth, fire, air and wind – all these he exhorted in his pure, childlike spirit to love God and to serve Him joyfully.
>
> He was wont to call all created things his brothers and sisters, and in a wonderful manner inaccessible to others he would enter into the secret of things as one to whom "the glorious liberty of the children of God" had been given.

The Christian nature mystic has seldom been described more felicitously than in the last few lines.

EDWARD ARMSTRONG

Sacramental Nature

from Saint Francis: Nature Mystic

It is not to minimize the achievement of Saint Francis but to place it within its setting to recognize that the intellectual and aesthetic milieu was at last such that his example of gaiety, asceticism, single-minded devotion to Christ, and sensitivity to Creation could appeal to pious, enterprising, and intelligent people. He enlarged their outlook by revealing the lark and the wild flower as sacramental and all nature singing out to man to join in adoration of the Creator. Unfortunately, controversy soon concentrated on the degree of honour due to Lady Poverty – to the neglect of the fair maiden Gaiety and bounteous Dame Nature.

EDWARD ARMSTRONG

The Voice of the Lord

from Lavengro

We went into the tent and sat down, and now the rain began to pour with vehemence. "I hope we shall not be flooded in this hollow," said I to Belle. "There is no fear of that," said Belle; "the wandering people, amongst other names, call it the dry hollow. I believe there is a passage somewhere or other by which the wet is carried off. There must be a cloud right above us, it is so dark. Oh! what a flash!"

"And what a peal," said I; "that is what the Hebrews call Koul Adonai – the voice of the Lord. Are you afraid?"

"No," said Belle, "I rather like to hear it."

"You are right," said I, "I am fond of the sound of thunder myself. There is nothing like it; Koul Adonai behadar; the voice of the Lord is a glorious voice, as the prayer-book version hath it."

"There is something awful in it," said Belle; "and then the lightning, the whole dingle is now in a blaze."

" 'The voice of the Lord maketh the hinds to calve, and discovereth the thick bushes.' As you say, there is something awful in thunder."

"There are all kinds of noises above us," said Belle; "surely I heard the crashing of a tree?"

" 'The voice of the Lord breaketh the cedar trees.' "

GEORGE BORROW (1803–1881)

I and My Rose

There is a world of wonder in this rose;
God made it, and his whole creation grows
To a point of perfect beauty
In this garden plot. He knows
The poet's thrill
On this June morning, as he sees
His will
To beauty taking form, his word
Made flesh, and dwelling among men.
All mysteries
In this one flower meet
And intertwine,
The universal is concrete
The human and divine,
In one unique and perfect thing, are fused
Into a unit of Love,
This rose as I behold it;
For all things gave it me,
The stars have helped to mould it,
The air, soft moonshine, and the rain,
The meekness of old mother earth,
The many-billowed sea.
The evolution of ten million years,
And all the pain
Of ages, brought it to its birth
And gave it me.
The tears
Of Christ are in it,
And his blood
Has dyed it red,

I could not see it but for him
Because he led
Me to the love of God,
From which all beauty springs.
I and my rose
Are one.

G. A. STUDDERT KENNEDY (1883–1929)

The Flower of the Fruit

In the silence of flowers is found a sacred love
That changes the future.
Being is, for its own road, the end
If some grace grants it
Fragrance and quiet.

Sweet blood explodes upon the tongue
When you break
The body of fruit:
This is the word, vivid and absolute
With which each tree tries out its virtue.

Man is mystic tree and barely grasps
Space and Time if he can turn himself
Into soul's flower and veins' fruit;

For, from his double essence, unconfused
The bees of death draw honey
And the roses of life their fragrance.

THOMAS MERTON (1915–1968)

Reciprocal Love

from Saint Francis: Nature Mystic

Coleridge in a later age experienced this sense of reciprocated love for nature and expressed it in imagery with religious nuances: "Even when all men have seemed to desert us, and the friend of our heart has passed on, with one glance from his 'cold, disliking eye' – yet even then the blue heaven spreads out and bends over us, and the little tree still shelters us under its plumage as a second cope, a domestic firmament, and the low-creeping gale will sigh in the heath-plant and soothe us by the sound of sympathy till the lulled grief lose itself in fixed gaze on the purple heath-blossom, till the present beauty becomes a vision of ecstasy."

Unless the heart is cold or alienated, even the ragged rocks do not reply merely with a barren echo to those who seek a path through them. They are found to be more than granite or sandstone, and the birds that nest there, the plants that cling to their clefts are seen to be, not only fascinating objects for the ornithologist, botanist, or artist but, as Saint Francis perceived, immanent with the life of God. Communion with nature, which may sometimes rise to ecstatic experience, sustains us because, as a pagan poet proclaimed and a Christian prophet endorsed, "In Him we live and move and have our being."

EDWARD ARMSTRONG

Neither Let It Be Fearful

Christmas 1938

I am the wind that blows
  The petal from the rose,
  And I the rose that mourns
  And dies upon the thorns;

I am the thorn that burns
  And unto dust returns,
  And I the dust wherefrom
  The rose again shall bloom.

He that shall know those thorns
  And feel that flame that burns,
  And touch that dust, and find
  Those petals on the wind,

And in the rose believe,
  He shall the rose achieve,
  The living rose, and know
  My love within him grow.

His heart shall have no fear
  Though from the shades appear
  Upon remorseless wings
  Inexorable things.

SIR ARTHUR FFORDE (1900–1985)

The Determination of love

from Love's Endeavour, Love's Expense

We have been describing a certain way of looking at the world of nature. It includes an awareness of the "rights" of nature, of the equilibrium of nature and of the patient inventiveness of nature. This way of looking at nature permits us to attach some meaning to the concept that the detail of nature may "come right" or "come wrong". Every commonplace detail of nature, every stone or tree, includes an immense richness and variety of lesser detail: in every fragment of it a thousand million lesser fragments cohere and interact. In every fragment of it, therefore, lie one hundred possibilities of "the one case in ten million" which is abnormal and aberrant, which fits no pattern and cannot be explained: and each of these hundred possibilities contains the threat of a distorted, stunted, diseased or barren tree. Where the threat is actualised, there perhaps stands such a tree; or perhaps there is no tree but only a decaying seed which never germinates; or perhaps out of the unusual distortion of the branches of the tree, a shape has been formed which is strangely beautiful against the winter sky. In the stunted tree we see the tragedy of nature "come wrong": in the shape on the skyline we see the tragedy of distortion redeemed into the triumph of beauty: in the being of this or any tree we see triumph over the possibility that there might be no tree at all. In the being of the tree we see triumph over the destructive potential of that one case in ten million which is the aberrant step of nature, the point where creativity has gone awry. Where the destructive potential is actualised, we see the tragedy of nature: and we also see, on occasion, that endless inventiveness of nature which, out of the material of tragedy, fashions the possibility of a new kind or level of triumph.

Tentatively, but with growing assurance, theology may interpret the dynamic of nature as the activity of love.

W. H. VANSTONE (1923–)

I Contemplate a Tree

from I and Thou

I contemplate a tree.

I can accept it as a picture: a rigid pillar in a flood of light, or splashes of green traversed by the gentleness of the blue silver ground.

I can feel it as movement: the flowing veins around the sturdy, striving core, the sucking of the roots, the breathing of the leaves, the infinite commerce with earth and air – and the growing itself in its darkness.

I can assign it to a species and observe it as an instance, with an eye to its construction and its way of life.

I can overcome its uniqueness and form so rigorously that I recognize it only as an expression of the law – those laws according to which a constant opposition of forces is continually adjusted, or those laws according to which the elements mix and separate.

I can dissolve it into a number, into a pure relation between numbers, and eternalize it.

Throughout all of this the tree remains my object and has its place and its time span, its kind and condition.

But it can also happen, if will and grace are joined, that as I contemplate the tree I am drawn into a relation, and the tree ceases to be an It. The power of exclusiveness has seized me.

This does not require me to forego any of the modes of contemplation. There is nothing that I must not see in order to see, and there is no knowledge that I must forget. Rather is everything, picture and movement, species and instance, law and number included and inseparably fused.

Whatever belongs to the tree is included: its form and its mechanics, its colors and its chemistry, its conversation with the elements and its conversation with the stars – all this in its entirety.

The tree is no impression, no play of my imagination, no

aspect of a mood; it confronts me bodily and has to deal with me as I must deal with it – only differently.

One should not try to dilute the meaning of the relation: relation is reciprocity.

Does the tree then have consciousness, similar to our own? I have no experience of that. But thinking that you have brought this off in your own case, must you again divide the indivisible? What I encounter is neither the soul of a tree nor a dryad, but the tree itself.

MARTIN BUBER (1878–1965)

The Clothing of God

from Mysticism

The mysterious vitality of trees, the silent magic of the forest, the strange and steady cycle of its life, possess in a peculiar degree this power of unleashing the human soul: are curiously friendly to its cravings, minister to its inarticulate needs. Unsullied by the corroding touch of consciousness, that life can make a contact with the "great life of the All"; and through its mighty rhythms man can receive a message concerning the true and timeless World of "all that is, and was, and evermore shall be." Plant life of all kinds, indeed, from the "flower in the crannied wall" to the "Woods of Westermain" can easily become, for selves of a certain type, a "mode of the Infinite." So obvious does this appear when we study the history of the mystics, that Steiner has drawn from it the hardly warrantable inference that "plants are just those natural phenomena whose qualities in the higher world are similar to their qualities in the physical world."

Though the conclusion be not convincing, the fact remains. The flowery garment of the world is for some mystics a medium of ineffable perception, a source of exalted joy, the veritable clothing of God. I need hardly add that such a state of things has always been found incredible by common sense. "The tree which moves some to tears of joy," says Blake, who possessed in an eminent degree this form of sacramental perception, "is in the Eyes of others only a green thing that stands in the Way."

EVELYN UNDERHILL (1875–1941)

The Cross Tree

Thou alone wast counted worthy
   this world's ranson to sustain,
that a shipwrecked race for ever
   might a port of refuge gain,
with the sacred blood anointed
   of the Lamb for sinners slain.

Faithful Cross, above all other,
   one and only noble tree,
none on foliage, none on blossom,
   none in fruit thy peer may be;
sweet the wood, and sweet the iron,
   and thy load, most sweet is he.

Bend, O lofty tree, thy branches,
   thy too rigid sinews bend;
and awhile the stubborn hardness,
   which thy birth bestowed, suspend;
and the limbs of heaven's high Monarch
   gently on thine arms extend.

FORTUNATUS (530–600)

Divine Happiness

from Aelred of Rievaulx

All these considerations separate God from his creatures, since
in him love is fulfilled and has nothing to seek. He does not
suffer from the hunger and thirst which, in one form or another,
is the mark of everything he has made. For if, from this vision
of pre-eminent selfgiving, unselfseeking charity in God, we
now descend to look closer at the creation, we begin to see
that every single thing, from the highest angel to the smallest
worm, has about it some reminiscence of the divine charity
which is as intimate to it as charity is to the life of God. For
all things are by nature so adjusted within themselves and
related to each other that nothing can be at peace out of its
appointed relation to other things. A stone thrown into the air
will fall back to earth, oil will rise to the surface of other liquids,
one tree will flourish only on heavy, another only on light and
sandy soil. Animal needs are more complex, but are still limited
to pursuing the satisfaction of the senses. Man alone strives
higher. He cannot rest in anything less than the divine
happiness itself, towards which a certain natural drive for ever
urges him on. Since nothing can destroy this desire, of which
everyone has interior evidence, there is no rest for man except
in attaining beautitude. This is the source of man's misery in
so far as, deluded by false appearances, he seeks his bliss where
it cannot be found. But it is also the source of his glory as a
rational being.

O wonderful creature, lower only than the creator, how do
you debase yourself? You love the world? But you are nobler
than the world. You wonder at the sun? But you are brighter
than the sun. You philosophize about the position of this
turning vault of heaven? Yet you are more sublime than
heaven. You search into the secret causes of creatures? Yet
there is no cause more secret than you. Why, then, pursue

fleeting beauty when your own beauty is not dimmed by old age or defiled by poverty, does not fade in sickness or perish even with death? Seek, by all means, seek what you are seeking, but do not seek it there.

Aelred's idea that man is driven by a natural urge for the divine happiness, for a good beyond all created good, has a long ancestry, and it is only one of the points in the *Mirror of Charity* at which the world of Plato's *Symposium* becomes again, in rather different guise, unexpectedly real. Aelred's is, naturally, a Platonism mediated by Augustine, but at moments re-felt and re-created with a surprising sureness. Like Augustine, Aelred thinks of love as, in itself, a morally uncommitted force, pre-supposed to that differentiation which makes it deviate into the vicious selfishness of cupidity or rise to the self-giving of true charity. It is simply man's share in the cosmic eros which is the inalienable mark of what it is to be a creature.

AELRED SQUIRE

A Figure of the All Thing

from Revelations of Divine Love

In this same time our Lord shewed me a spiritual sight of His homely loving.

I saw that He is to us everything that is good and comfortable for us: He is our clothing that for love wrappeth us, claspeth us, and all encloseth us for tender love, that He may never leave us; being to us all-thing that is good, as to mine understanding.

Also in this He shewed me a little thing, the quantity of an hazel-nut, in the palm of my hand; and it was as round as a ball. I looked thereupon with eye of my understanding, and thought: *What may this be?* And it was answered generally thus: *It is all that is made.* I marvelled how it might last, for methought it might suddenly have fallen to naught for little. And I was answered in my understanding: *It lasteth, and ever shall for that God loveth it.* And so All-thing hath the Being by the love of God.

In this Little Thing I saw three properties. The first is that God made it, the second is that God loveth it, the third, that God keepeth it. But what is to me verily the Maker, the Keeper, and the Lover, – I cannot tell; for till I am Substantially oned to Him, I may never have full rest nor very bliss: that is to say, till I be so fastened to Him, that there is right nought that is made betwixt my God and me.

JULIAN OF NORWICH (c. 1342–1413)

The Spiritual in the Earthly

from Searchings in the Silence

"Supposing Him to be the gardener." John 20:15

We often mistake Christ for the gardener – attribute to mere physical beauty what comes from faith alone. We speak of the glories of Nature; most of its glories belong to man. We find a sense of infinitude in the breath of the new-mown hay; yet, truly, it is not in that, but in *thee*. It has been said: "Thou weavest for God the garment by which thou seest Him"; more justly might the words be spoken of Nature. Her song is the echo of thy song. She answers in refrain to thee – to thy sorrows and to thy joys. Often have men exhorted thee to follow the teachings of Nature, and to look on the things beyond as an idle dream. Nay, but thy vision of Nature depends on thy vision of grace.

In vain shalt thou seek in the flower the grace which is not in thy soul. It is from the things beyond the earth that earthly beauty flows. The voice which thou hearest in the garden is the voice of the Lord. That which uplifts thee in the flower is just what the gardener has not planted. It is the life below the stem, the mystery beneath the root. It is the sense of a presence which has escaped the eye, of a power which has eluded the botanist. It is the feeling that the gardener has planted something which he has not seen – a seed from the life eternal, a blossom from the breast of God.

Oh, Thou, whose Easter morning shines in many disguises, help me to recognize Thee everywhere. Let me not ascribe to the gardener the work that is done by Thee. I often speak of the noble lives led by men who do not know Thee; teach me that Thou knowest *them*. Tell me that Thy presence is wider than our creed, Thy temple bigger than our sanctuary, Thy love larger than our law. Convince me that Thou enfoldest that which does not enfold *Thee*. Let me learn that Thou art the one "excellent name in all the earth". Men call their excellent things by other names; they take Thee to be the gardener. Hasten the time when they shall take the gardener to be Thee; they shall be nearer to the truth of things. Hasten the time when "in the flesh they shall see God" – see Him in the forms of earth, see Him in the duties of the hour, see Him in the paths of life, see Him in the progress of the day. Make Thyself known to them in the breaking of the earthly bread; in the planting of the earthly flower let them gaze on *Thee.*

GEORGE MATHESON (1842–1906)

Prayer

To Thee Whom I do not and cannot know, – within me and beyond me – and to Whom I am bound by love, fear and faith – to the One and to the Many – I address this prayer:

"Guide me to my better self – help me make myself into one who is trusted by living things, creatures and plants, as well as the air, water, earth and light that sustain these, keep me as one who respects the mystery and the character of every variety of life in both its uniqueness and its mass, for all life is essential to its own survival.

"Help me to preserve my capacity for wonder, ecstasy and discovery, allow me everywhere to awaken the sense of beauty, and with and for others and for myself to contribute to the sum of beauty we behold, we hear, we smell, taste or touch or are otherwise aware of through mind and spirit; help me never to lose the life-giving exercise of protecting all that breathes and thirsts and hungers; all that suffers.

"Help me find a balance between the longer rewards and the shorter pleasures, while remaining in tune with relative values, while patiently according the passage of time its rich harvest of loyalties, experience, achievement, support and inspiration.

"Help me be a good trustee for the body You gave me. No life is to do with as I will, not even my own, for it is like an object entrusted into my temporary keeping, to bequeath back into the earthly cycle in the best possible condition for other life to continue.

"Therefore, Thy will be done."

YEHUDI MENUHIN (1916–)

The Religious Response

The Religious Response

Men and women have in all ages and places been moved by reverence and awe to worship God. The authors here come from a specifically Christian tradition. Some, like W. H. Hudson and Jack Clemo, are critical of the Church. Others such as Saint Patrick, George Herbert, John Keble and Helmut Thielicke belong to its official ministry. All agree that you cannot make religion a private matter between God and man.

For many Christians an appreciation of the natural world has enlarged and deepened their faith. When eyes are open to God, the world seems to take on a new beauty.

Like the lover who sees his beloved in everything, so a heart opened to the love of God sees him everywhere, and longs that others might love him too.

The Oxen

Christmas Eve, and twelve of the clock,
  "Now they are all on their knees,"
An elder said as we sat in a flock
  By the embers in hearthside ease.

We pictured the meek mild creatures where
  They dwelt in their strawy pen,
Nor did it occur to one of us there
  To doubt they were kneeling then.

So fair a fancy few would weave
  In these years! Yet, I feel,
If someone said on Christmas Eve,
  "Come; see the oxen kneel

"In the lonely barton by yonder coomb
  Our childhood used to know,"
I should go with him in the gloom,
  Hoping it might be so.

THOMAS HARDY (1840–1928)

Kneeling

Moments of great calm,
Kneeling before an altar
Of wood in a stone church
In summer, waiting for the God
To speak: the air a staircase
For silence; the sun's light
Ringing me, as though I acted
A great role. And the audiences
Still; all that close throng
Of spirits waiting, as I,
For the message.
             Prompt me, God;
But not yet. When I speak,
Though it be you who speak
Through me, something is lost.
The meaning is in the waiting.

R. S. THOMAS (1913–)

Benedicite

O all ye Works of the Lord, bless ye the Lord: praise him, and magnify him for ever.

O ye Angels of the Lord, bless ye the Lord: praise him, and magnify him for ever.

O ye Heavens, bless ye the Lord: praise him, and magnify him for ever.

O ye Waters that be above the Firmament, bless ye the Lord: praise him, and magnify him for ever.

O all ye Powers of the Lord, bless ye the Lord: praise him, and magnify him for ever.

O ye Sun, and Moon, bless ye the Lord: praise him, and magnify him for ever.

O ye Stars of Heaven, bless ye the Lord: praise him, and magnify him for ever.

O ye Showers, and Dew, bless ye the Lord: praise him, and magnify him for ever.

O ye Winds of God, bless ye the Lord: praise him, and magnify him for ever.

O ye Fire and Heat, bless ye the Lord: praise him and magnify him for ever.

O ye Winter and Summer, bless ye the Lord: praise him, and magnify him for ever.

O ye Dews, and Frosts, bless ye the Lord: praise him, and magnify him for ever.

O ye Frost and Cold, bless ye the Lord: praise him, and magnify him for ever.

O ye Ice and Snow, bless ye the Lord: praise him, and magnify him for ever.

O ye Nights, and Days, bless ye the Lord: praise him, and magnify him for ever.

O ye Light and Darkness, bless ye the Lord: praise him, and magnify him for ever.

O ye Lightnings, and Clouds, bless ye the Lord: praise him, and magnify him for ever.

O let the Earth bless the Lord: yea, let it praise him, and magnify him for ever.

O ye Mountains, and Hills, bless ye the Lord: praise him, and magnify him for ever.

O all ye Green Things upon the Earth, bless ye the Lord: praise him, and magnify him for ever.

O ye Wells, bless ye the Lord: praise him, and magnify him for ever.

O ye Seas, and Floods, bless ye the Lord: praise him, and magnify him for ever.

O ye Whales, and all that move in the Waters, bless ye the Lord: praise him, and magnify him for ever.

O all ye Fowls of the Air, bless ye the Lord: praise him, and magnify him for ever.

O all ye Beasts, and Cattle, bless ye the Lord: praise him, and magnify him for ever.

O ye Children of Men, bless ye the Lord: praise him, and magnify him for ever.

O let Israel bless the Lord: praise him, and magnify him for ever.

O ye Priests of the Lord, bless ye the Lord: praise him, and magnify him for ever.

O ye Servants of the Lord, bless ye the Lord: praise him, and magnify him for ever.

O ye Spirits and Souls of the Righteous, bless ye the Lord: praise him, and magnify him for ever.

O ye holy and humble Men of heart, bless ye the Lord: praise him, and magnify him for ever.

Canticle of the Sun

All creatures of our God and King,
lift up your voice and with us sing
  Alleluia, alleluia.
Thou burning sun with golden beam,
thou silver moon with softer gleam,
  O praise him, O praise him,
  Alleluia, alleluia, alleluia.

Thou rushing wind that art so strong,
ye clouds that sail in heaven along,
  O praise him, alleluia.
Thou rising morn, in praise rejoice,
ye lights of evening, find a voice;

Thou flowing water, pure and clear,
make music for thy Lord to hear,
  Alleluia, alleluia.
Thou fire so masterful and bright,
that givest man both warmth and light:

Dear mother earth, who day by day
unfoldest blessings on our way,
  O praise him, alleluia.
The flowers and fruits that in thee grow,
let them his glory also show:

W. H. DRAPER (1855–1933)
after SAINT FRANCIS

The Chorus of Praise

from Man and the Natural World

All animals were thought to have religious instincts. Classical authors taught that fowls had "a certain ceremonious religion" and that elephants adored the moon. Such traditions were easily Christianized. Psalm 148 declared that all creatures praised the Lord, even "beasts and all cattle; creeping things and flying fowl". "Let man and beast appear before him, and magnify his name together," sang Christopher Smart. Some theologians, and many poets, regarded bird-song as a kind of hymn-singing. "The wren and the robin . . . sing a treble," wrote Bishop Goodman in 1624, "the goldfinch, the nightingale, they join in the mean; the blackbirds, they bear the tenor, while the four-footed beasts with their bleating and bellowing they sing a bass."

KEITH THOMAS (1933–)

The Duet with the Nightingale

from Saint Francis: Nature Mystic

The motif of man and bird praising God together reached its highest refinement in a story that belongs to a time subsequent to Celano's biographies and may well be of later date than the *Fioretti*. While Saint Francis and Brother Leo were enjoying a meal together in the open air, they were delighted by the singing of a nightingale close by. Francis suggested: "Let us sing the praise of God antiphonally with this bird." Leo excused himself as he was no singer, but the saint lifted up his voice and phrase by phrase sang alternately with the nightingale. So they continued from Vespers to Lauds until Francis at last admitted defeat. Then the nightingale took wing and fluttered to his hand, where he fed it, praising it enthusiastically. He gave the small brown songster his blessing, and it flew off into the bushes.

EDWARD ARMSTRONG

The Necessity of Choice

from How the World Began

What Däubler is saying is that men, you and I, are not merely "shone upon" by God's light, as are the other creatures, like trees, animals, and houses; rather we men are "addressed" by the Word of God. When the Word of God is beamed upon us, do we then light up? No, it is terrible to say, man can remain in the dark nevertheless. We can withhold ourselves from this Word. But there is one thing we cannot do. We cannot evade the decision whether we shall stand beneath this Word or whether we shall desire to be our own masters. Once this Word has struck us we are involved in an encounter with God which we cannot escape. We must say either Yes or No to him.

HELMUT THIELICKE (1908–)

Virtue

Sweet day, so cool, so calm, so bright!
The bridal of the earth and sky –
The dew shall weep thy fall to-night;
    For thou must die.

Sweet rose, whose hue angry and brave
Bids the rash gazer wipe his eye,
Thy root is ever in its grave,
    And thou must die.

Sweet spring, full of sweet days and roses,
A box where sweets compacted lie,
My music shows ye have your closes,
    And all must die.

Only a sweet and virtuous soul,
Like season'd timber, never gives;
But though the whole world turn to coal,
    Then chiefly lives.

GEORGE HERBERT (1593–1632)

Providence

The Country Parson, considering the great aptness Country people have to think that all things come by a kind of natural course; and that if they sow and soil their grounds, they must have corn; if they keep and fodder well their cattle, they must have milk, and Calves; labours to reduce them to see God's hand in all things, and to believe, that things are not set in such an inevitable order, but that God often changeth it according as he sees fit, either for reward or punishment.

By God's *governing power* he preserves and orders the references of things one to the other, so that though the corn do grow, and be preserved in that act by his *sustaining power*, yet if he suit not other things to the growth, as seasons, and weather, and other accidents, by his *governing power*, the fairest harvests come to nothing. And it is observable, that God delights to have men feel, and acknowledge, and reverence his power, and therefore he often overturns things, when they are thought past danger; that is his time of interposing: As when a Merchant hath a ship come home after many a storm, which it hath escaped, he destroys it sometimes in the very Haven; or if the goods be housed, a fire hath broken forth, and suddenly consumed them. Now this he doth, that men should perpetuate, and not break off their acts of dependence, how fair soever the opportunities present themselves. So that if a Farmer should depend upon God all the year, and being ready to put hand to sickle, shall then secure himself, and think all cock sure; then God sends such weather, as lays the corn, and destroys it: or if he depend on God further, even till he imbarn his corn, and then think all sure; God sends a fire and consumes all that he hath: For that he ought not to break off, but to continue his dependence on God, not only before the corn is inned, but after also; and, indeed, to depend, and fear continually.

The third power is spiritual, by which God turns all outward blessings to inward advantages. So that if a Farmer hath both a fair harvest, and that also well inned, and imbarned, and continuing safe there; yet if God give him not the Grace to use and utter this well, all his advantages are to his loss. Better were his corn burnt, than not spiritually improved. And it is observable in this, how God's goodness strives with man's refractoriness; Man would sit down at this world, God bids him fell it, and purchase a better: Just as a Father who hath in his hand an apple, and a piece of gold under it; the Child comes, and with pulling, gets the apple out of his Father's hand: his Father bids him throw it away, and he will give him the gold for it, which the Child utterly refusing, eats it, and is troubled with worms: So is the carnal and wilful man with the worm of the grave in this world, and the worm of Conscience in the next.

GEORGE HERBERT (1593–1632)

Evening Hymn

The duteous day now closeth,
each flower and tree reposeth,
    shade creeps o'er wild and wood:
let us, as night is falling,
on God our maker calling,
    give thanks to him, the giver good.

Now all the heavenly splendour
breaks forth in starlight tender
    from myriad worlds unknown;
and man, the marvel seeing,
forgets his selfish being,
    for joy of beauty not his own.

ROBERT BRIDGES (1844–1930)

Faith and Penitence

After all these intercessions for others and prayers for spiritual good, comes in one short prayer for the things needful to our temporal and earthly life. "That it may please Thee to give and preserve to our use the kindly fruits of the earth, so as in due time we may enjoy them." Whereby we are taught the same lesson as in the Lord's prayer: "Give us this day our daily bread:" which words not coming in till we are half way through the prayer, shew us that we are not to make so very much of the good things of this world, in comparison of the better things of heaven. At the same time we are instructed to depend not on our own skill and industry but on the blessing of our Creator both for the growth and preservation of the fruits of the earth, and for our enjoyment of them.

But what is this which comes in at the end of all? "That it may please Thee to give us true repentance:"

JOHN KEBLE (1792–1866)

The Sower and the Seed

In the first place, the mere act of putting the seed into the
ground is a lesson from Almighty God, to put us in mind of
the fall of our first parents, and our sad condition in consequence of it. Before Adam fell, as you know, the Lord God
Himself planted the trees upon the fruit whereof Adam was to
live; no need for Adam to sow or set them in the ground, God
caused them to grow there (as men speak) of their own accord:
"every tree that was pleasant to the sight and good for food."
Adam had indeed to dress and keep the garden, but it was not
in the way of toil or hard work: it was rather, as we may believe,
in the way of service done to Almighty God the Owner of the
garden; it was pleasurable exercise, not wearisome trouble: and
having done so, he had but to put forth his hand, and take of
all trees but one, and freely eat. But when they had unhappily
listened to the enemy – when lust had brought sin, and sin
death – all this as you know was changed; the sentence went
out immediately, "Cursed is the ground:" and ever since the
rule of this world has been, "In the sweat of thy face shalt thou
eat bread." The ground, left to itself, as we all know, brings
forth only thorns and thistles, nettles and all manner of weeds
and rubbish: if you want good food out of it, "Wine that maketh
glad the heart of man, and oil to make his face to shine, and
bread which strengtheneth man's heart," there must be ploughing, raking and harrowing, planting and sowing, fencing and
weeding, and all the hard and anxious work of the farm and
garden. And why should it be so? What reason is there in the
nature of things, why a piece of ground left to itself should not
bear wheat and barley, vines or good fruits, as well as nettles
and brambles and all manner of weeds? You never can find
any reason, but this one, that it so pleased God. It pleased God
that the ground so left to itself without any sort of cultivation,
should not ordinarily bring forth the food that is needed for
man's life. And why? For a token to us all how displeasing
sin is to God: for a remembrance of His curse laid upon the

earth for the first sinner's sake. That curse is not worn out: this world indeed appears to grow on the whole, outwardly and bodily, more and more comfortable to live in, as fresh contrivances are found out, and civilization, as it is called, goes on: but still each new generation finds, as the former generation had done, that the old sentence remains, man's life must be labour and sorrow. Earth, left to itself, will not feed him.

JOHN KEBLE (1792–1866)

Harvest Psalm

Psalm 65: 9–14

Thou visitest the earth, and blessest it: thou makest it very plenteous.

The river of God is full of water: thou preparest their corn, for so thou providest for the earth.

Thou waterest her furrows, thou sendest rain into the little valleys thereof: thou makest it soft with the drops of rain, and blessest the increase of it.

Thou crownest the year with thy goodness: and thy clouds drop fatness.

They shall drop upon the dwellings of the wilderness: and the little hills shall rejoice on every side.

The folds shall be full of sheep: the valleys also shall stand so thick with corn, that they shall laugh and sing.

True Reverence

from Afoot in England

The fun over, I went soberly back to my village, and finding it impossible to get to sleep I went to Sunday-morning service at Shrewton Church. It was strangely restful there after that noisy morning crowd at Stonehenge. The church is white stone with Norman pillars and old oak beams laid over the roof painted or distempered blue – a quiet, peaceful blue. There was also a good deal of pleasing blue colour in the glass of the east window. The service was, as I almost invariably find it in a village church, beautiful and impressive. Listening to the music of prayer and praise, with some natural outdoor sound to fill up the pauses – the distant crow of a cock or the song of some bird close by – a corn-bunting or wren or hedge-sparrow – and the bright sunlight filling the interior, I felt as much refreshed as if kind Nature's sweet restorer, balmy sleep, had visited me that morning. The sermon was nothing to me; I scarcely heard it, but understood that it was about the Incarnation and the perfection of the Higher Criticism and of all who doubt because they do not understand. I remembered vaguely that on three successive Sundays in three village churches in the wilds of Wiltshire I had heard sermons preached on and against the Higher Criticism. I thought it would have been better in this case if the priest had chosen to preach on Stonehenge and had said that he devoutly wished we were sun-worshippers, like the Persians as well as Christians; also that we were Buddhists, and worshippers of our dead ancestors like the Chinese, and that we were pagans and idolators who bow down to sticks and stones, if all these added cults would serve to make us more reverent. And I wish he could have said that it was as irreligious to go to Stonehenge, that ancient temple which man raised to the unknown god thousands of years ago, to indulge in noise and horseplay at the hour of sunrise, as it would be to go to Salisbury Cathedral for such a purpose.

W. H. HUDSON (1841–1922)

Easter Day 1870

The happiest, brightest, most beautiful Easter I have ever spent. I woke early and looked out. As I had hoped the day was cloudless, a glorious morning. My first thought was "Christ is Risen". It is not well to lie in bed on Easter morning, indeed it is thought very unlucky. I got up between five and six and was out soon after six. There had been a frost and the air was rimy with a heavy thick white dew on hedge, bank and turf, but the morning was not cold. There was a heavy white dew with a touch of hoar frost on the meadows, and as I leaned over the wicket gate by the mill pond looking to see if there were any primroses in the banks but not liking to venture into the dripping grass suddenly I heard the cuckoo for the first time this year. He was near Peter's Pool and he called three times quickly one after another. It is very well to hear the cuckoo for the first time on Easter Sunday morning. I loitered up the lane again gathering primroses.

The village lay quiet and peaceful in the morning sunshine, but by the time I came back from primrosing there was some little stir and people were beginning to open their doors and look out into the fresh fragrant splendid morning.

There was a very large congregation at morning church, the largest I have seen for some time, attracted by Easter and the splendour of the day, for they have here an immense reverence for Easter Sunday. The anthem went very well and Mr Baskerville complimented Mr Evans after church about it, saying that it was sung in good tune and time and had been a great treat. There were more communicants than usual: twenty-nine. This is the fifth time I have received the Sacrament within four days. After morning service I took Mr V. round the churchyard and showed him the crosses on his mother's, wife's, and brother's graves. He was quite taken by surprise and very much gratified. I am glad to see that our primrose crosses seem to be having some effect for I think I notice this Easter some attempt to copy them and an advance towards the form of the cross in some of the decorations of the graves. I wish we could get the people to adopt some little design in the disposition of the flowers upon the graves instead of sticking sprigs into the turf aimlessly anywhere, anyhow and with no meaning at all. But one does not like to interfere too much with their artless, natural way of showing their respect and love for the dead. I am thankful to find this beautiful custom on the increase, and observed more and more every year. Some years ago it was on the decline and nearly discontinued. On Easter Day all the young people come out in something new and bright like butterflies. It is almost part of their religion to wear something new on this day. It was an old saying that if you don't wear something new on Easter Day, the crows will spoil everything you have on.

Between the services a great many people were in the churchyard looking at the graves. I went to Bettws Chapel in the afternoon. It was burning hot and as I climbed the hill the perspiration rolled off my forehead from under my hat and fell in drops on the dusty road. Lucretia Wall was in chapel looking pale and pretty after her illness. Coming down the hill it was delightful, cool and pleasant. The sweet suspicion of spring strengthens, deepens, and grows more sweet every day. Mrs Pring gave us lamb and asparagus at dinner.

FRANCIS KILVERT (1840–1879)

Sermon on Grass

One sermon so much impressed Kathleen that her father bade her write it out – old Job's sermon on grass. Job was one of the few labouring members of the Wesleyan community, a great-grandson of one of the founders of the chapel. He was a shepherd and no appearance could have been more suitable than his for his office. He was of the long type – tall, with long face, long hands. His old clothes hung loosely about him. His face had the look of one who sympathises and weighs, and the quickly shifting expression of almost excessive sensitiveness. Among the spruce tradesmen and well-clad young farmers his looks had become remarkable.

"This is harvest time, but I won't talk to you about harvest . . . I'm going to talk about grass. Here's my text: just 'The grass of the field.' You know how the full text goes. God cared for grass so as to clothe it wi' beauty and adorn it wi' flowers.

"The pity of it is that the Bible wasn't written in a beautiful grassy country, not as I gather. Perhaps it wouldn't ha' done for Christ to walk too often up our hills in Spring. He'd not perhaps ha' thought we needed his salvation and we'd have had maybe only a Nature worship, and that for such as us is not enough. But it does me good to think of Him looking down on our ground. Beauty he loved, an' I don't doubt it lightened his suffering. There's no daisies, nor yet celandines in the Bible, not even in the Psalms. And yet it's a sight most freshening to the mind in Spring to look down the fields in this and Oxhill parish and see the daisies on the crowns of the old broad plough ridges and the celandines in the hollows between.

"They wouldn't be there if we was to drain better, but out of ruinous farming comes the shining gold of celandines. But that's going back to the Spring of the year, which with Autumn on us, I shouldn't. Only I love to compare the seasons. The softness of this September mixes well in the mind with the blustering winds of March. And the smell of the walnut hoods challenges a body, can he remember the smell of the may and the lilac? But I am forgetting. I'm talking o' grass. Of all the natural gifts of God I thought of grass to talk about. Grass is always with us. It never fails us, even in the farming sense. It clothes the whole world as with a cloak. It feeds the beasts and they feed us. Permanent grass is a rest for the thoughts. 'I lay me down in green pastures.' The green colour o' grass rests the eye, the never failingness of it rests the anxious mind; and the feel of it is rest for the body in summer season.

"The Bible says of the Spring grass 'The tender grass showeth itself.' Tender -- that is the word. Tender green to the eye, tender to the jaws of the young calves just turned out. The tender grass. There's one text that dooant seem to spake well o' grass. 'The grass withereth.' If everything withered as sweet as grass, 'twould be a good world. The grass that withers standing makes a fine music in the wind, though it takes a fine ear to hear it. And have y'ever sin the red sunset reflected on a million shinin' dry bents in autumn? It's a sight I can't talk about: but you may look for it in August when the sun's rays come level wi' the ground, out of a red sunset. I mind I see it every night o' that week when my bwoy came back from the war, back home to die. A man's eyes and ears be sharp when his blessings be slipping away.

"Ay, but that reminds me, grass robs death of its terrors for who but feels soothed at the thought of the green grass waving over a body that is weary and hurt, and laden with hard and painful memories? When I was young my thoughts would be too much for me and I'd long to be beneath the daisies; not up in heaven. For that you want newness of spirit. But God in his mercy lets us throw off our weariness and leave it kindly buried beneath the grinsw'd.

"What I really want to say is – look around you at the common mercies of the Lord. There's trees; there's bread and I'm saving up a sermon for you about little childer – all things that be around us now and always.

Count your blessings,
Name them one by one,
And it will surprise you
What the Lord hath done.''

JOSEPH ASHBY (1859–1919)

Grass

from Modern Painters

Consider a little what a depth there is in this great instinct of the human race. Gather a single blade of grass, and examine for a minute, quietly, its narrow sword-shaped strip of fluted green. Nothing, as it seems there, of notable goodness or beauty. A very little strength, and a very little tallness, and a few delicate long lines meeting in a point, – not a perfect point neither, but blunt and unfinished, by no means a creditable or apparently much cared-for example of Nature's workmanship; made, as it seems, only to be trodden on to-day, and to-morrow to be cast into the oven; and a little pale and hollow stalk, feeble and flaccid, leading down to the dull brown fibres of roots. And yet, think of it well, and judge whether of all the gorgeous flowers that beam in summer air, and of all strong and goodly trees, pleasant to the eyes or good for food, – stately palm and pine, strong ash and oak, scented citron, burdened vine, – there be any by man so deeply loved, by God so highly graced, as that narrow point of feeble green . . . And well does it fulfil its mission. Consider what we owe merely to the meadow grass, to the covering of the dark ground by that glorious enamel, by the companies of these soft, and countless, and peaceful spears. The fields! Follow but forth for a little time the thoughts of all that we ought to recognize in those words. All spring and summer is in them, – the walks by silent, scented paths, – the rest in noonday heat, – the joy of herds and flocks, – the power of all shepherd life and meditation, – the life of sunlight upon the world, falling in emerald streaks, and failing in soft blue shadows, where else it would have struck upon the dark mould, or scorching dust, – pastures beside the pacing brooks, – soft banks and knolls of lowly hills, – thyme slopes of down overlooked by the blue line of lifted sea, – crisp lawns all dim with early dew, or smooth in evening warmth of barred sunshine, dinted by happy feet, and softening in their fall the sound of loving voices: all these are summed in those simple words; and these are not all. We may not measure to the full the depth of this heavenly gift in our own land; though still, as we think of it longer, the infinite of that meadow sweetness, Shakspere's peculiar joy, would open on us more and more, yet we have it but in part. Go out, in the spring-time, among the meadows that slope from the shores of the Swiss lakes to the roots of their lower mountains. There, mingled with the taller gentians and the white narcissus, the grass grows deep and free; and as you follow the winding mountain paths, beneath arching boughs all veiled and dim with blossom, – paths that for ever droop and rise over the green banks and mounds sweeping down in scented undulation, steep to the blue water, studded here and there with new-mown heaps, filling all the air with fainter sweetness, – look up towards the higher hills, where the waves of everlasting green roll silently into their long inlets among the shadows of the pines; and we may, perhaps, at last know the meaning of those quiet words of the 147th Psalm, "He maketh grass to grow upon the mountains."

JOHN RUSKIN (1819–1900)

The Eyes of All Look to Him

from a Sermon: How the World Began

So Noah knows that he is safe with God even in *external* things. He knows that God undoubtedly has control over this catastrophic Flood.

Is it true that faith in God provides only an *inner* support? Many people believe this. They say that religion is a very good and practical thing in life. Religion provides strength and creates spiritual reserves which enable us to bear more easily the hard things in life. Well, people who think in this way are not counting upon the living God at all, even though this may sound quite devout. For this God of ours is not merely the Lord of our spiritual stirrings and emotions; he is the Master of fate itself. He not only gives us the "inner" courage, the mental and spiritual attitude, so to speak, in which we endure a dreadful illness, but he can also heal us of the illness itself. He not only gives us something like calmness of spirit when the little ship of our life is pitched to and fro in the storms; he needs only to speak *one* word and the waves are stilled – the actual, *external* waves, not merely the waves in our soul and the fevered beating of our heart.

In this very same way he not only gives "peace of soul" to Noah in his ark, but also sees to it that the flood cannot harm him. He also took in hand his *outward* fate.

I find it wonderfully good and comforting that here God is at work in a really "outward" way, completely outside any religious, spiritual, "inward" sphere whatsoever, that he is also with dogs and cats and elephants and wrens, who cannot have such a thing as a mental attitude or courage, and that he rejoices when the evening praise of Noah's family rings out across the desolate wastes mingled with barking, mewing, trumpeting, and warbling.

Nor should we drive our animals from the room when we have our family worship. After all, God is by no means so "spiritual" that he will associate only with men and, if possible, only with pious, spiritual-minded and highly moral men. After all, "the eyes of *all* look to him" and "out of the mouths of babes," out of the song of the lark and the croaking of frogs has he brought perfect praise.

So the ark went floating along, both men and beasts singing the praise of the Creator. For God loves every living thing.

HELMUT THIELICKE (1908–)

The Lord is my Shepherd

Psalm 23 : 1–6

The Lord is my shepherd: therefore can I lack nothing.

He shall feed me in a green pasture: and lead me forth beside the waters of comfort.

He shall convert my soul: and bring me forth in the paths of righteousness, for his Name's sake.

Yea, though I walk through the valley of the shadow of death,

I will fear no evil: for thou art with me; thy rod and thy staff comfort me.

Thou shalt prepare a table before me against them that trouble me: thou hast anointed my head with oil, and my cup shall be full.

But thy loving-kindness and mercy shall follow me all the days of my life: and I will dwell in the house of the Lord for ever.

Loves Birth

from Piers the Ploughman

There is a natural knowledge in your heart, which prompts you to love your Lord better than yourself and to die rather than commit mortal sin. That, surely, is Truth. If anyone else can teach you better, listen, and learn accordingly.

For this is the testimony of God's word, the word by which you must live: that Love is Heaven's sovereign remedy, and he who takes it has no trace of sin left. By Love, God chose to fashion all His works. He taught Moses that it was the dearest of all things, the virtue closest to Heaven, the plant of Peace whose leaves are most precious for healing.

Heaven could not hold Love, it was so heavy in itself. But when it had eaten its fill of earth, and taken flesh and blood, then it was lighter than a leaf on a linden-tree, more subtle and piercing than the point of a needle. The strongest armour was not proof against it, the tallest ramparts could not keep it out.

Therefore Love is first among the company of the Lord of Heaven; He is a mediator between God and man, as a Mayor is between king and people: He alone delivers judgement on man for his misdeeds, and assesses the penalties.

And so that one can recognize love by natural instinct, it begins by some power whose source and centre is in the heart of man. For every virtue springs from a natural knowledge in the heart, implanted there by the Father who created us – He who looked upon us with love and let His Son die for our sins, wishing no evil to those who tortured Him and put Him to death, but praying for their forgiveness.

WILLIAM LANGLAND (1330?–1400?)

I See His Blood

I see His blood upon the rose
And in the stars the glory of His eyes,
His body gleams amid eternal snows,
His tears fall from the skies.

I see His face in every flower;
The thunder and the singing of the birds
Are but His voice – and carven by His power
Rocks are His written words.

All pathways by His feet are worn,
His strong heart stirs the ever-beating sea,
His crown of thorns is twined with every thorn,
His cross is every tree.

JOSEPH M. PLUNKETT (1887–1916)

Christ in the Clay-pit

Why should I find Him here
And not in a church, nor yet
Where Nature heaves a breast like Olivet
Against the stars? I peer
Upon His footsteps in this quarried mud;
I see His blood
In rusty stains on pit-props, wagon-frames
Bristling with nails, not leaves: There were no leaves
Upon His chosen Tree,
No parasitic flowering over shames
Of Eden's primal infidelity.

Just splintered wood and nails
Were fairest blossoming for Him Who speaks
Where mica-silt outbreaks
Like water from the side of His own clay
In that strange day
When He was pierced. Here still the earth-face pales
And rends in earthquake roarings of a blast
With tainted rock outcast

While fields and woods lie dreaming yet of peace
'Twix God and His creation, of release
From potent wrath – a faith that waxes bold
In churches nestling snugly in the fold
Of scented hillsides where mild shadows brood.
The dark and stubborn mood
Of Him Whose feet are bare upon this mire,
And in the furnace fire
Which hardens all the clay that has escaped,
Would not be understood
By worshippers of beauty toned and shaped
To flower or hymn. I know their facile praise
False to the heart of me, which like this pit

Must still be disembowelled of Nature's stain,
And rendered fit
By violent mouldings through the tunnelled ways
Of all He would regain.

JACK CLEMO (1916–)

Turn Our Captivity

Psalm 126 : 5–7

Turn our captivity, O Lord: as the rivers in the south.

They that sow in tears: shall reap in joy.

He that now goeth on his way weeping, and beareth forth good seed: shall doubtless come again with joy, and bring his sheaves with him.

Indian Jesus

The face of Jesus lovely as the moon,
His mouth like a well-ripened scarlet fruit,
His eyes pouring forth love and grace,
His glowing body and his feet pink like the Lotus –
The desire to see all these burns within me.
Open wide the door of Heaven
Suffer me to behold him.

KRISHNA PILLAI (1827–1900)

Immanence

I come in little things,
Saith the Lord:
Not borne on morning wings
Of majesty, but I have set My feet
Amidst the delicate and bladed wheat
That springs triumphant in the furrowed sod.
There do I dwell, in weakness and in power;
Not broken or divided, saith our God!
In your strait garden plot I come to flower:
About your porch My Vine
Meek, fruitful, doth entwine;
Waits, at the threshold, Love's appointed hour.

I come in little things,
Saith the Lord:
Yea! on the glancing wings
Of eager birds, the softly pattering feet
Of furred and gentle beasts, I come to meet
Your hard and wayward hearts. In brown, bright eyes
That peep from out the brake I stand confest.
On every nest
Where feathery Patience is content to brood
And leaves her pleasure for the high emprize
Of motherhood –
There doth My Godhead rest.

I come in little things,
Saith the Lord:
My starry wings
I do forsake
Love's highway of humility to take:
Meekly I fit my stature to your need.
In beggar's part
About your gates I shall not cease to plead –

As man, to speak with man –
Till by such art
I shall achieve My Immemorial Plan
Pass the low lintel of the human heart.

EVELYN UNDERHILL (1875–1941)

The Watered Garden

Isaiah 58: 10–12

If you pour yourself out for the hungry
   and satisfy the desire of the afflicted,
then shall your light rise in the darkness
   and your gloom be as the noonday.
And the LORD will guide you continually,
   and satisfy your desire with good things,
   and make your bones strong;
and you shall be like a watered garden,
   like a spring of water,
   whose waters fail not.
And your ancient ruins shall be rebuilt;
   you shall raise up the foundations of many
      generations;
you shall be called the repairer of the breach,
   the restorer of streets to dwell in.

Hymn of the Universe

When your presence, Lord, has flooded me with its light I hoped that within it I might find ultimate reality at its most tangible.

But now that I have in fact laid hold on you, you who are utter consistency, and feel myself borne by you, I realize that my deepest hidden desire was not to possess you but to be possessed.

It is not as a radiation of light nor as subtilized matter that I desire you; nor was it thus that I described you in my first intuitive encounter with you: it was as fire. And I can see I shall have no rest unless an active influence, coming forth from you, bears down on me to transform me.

The whole universe is aflame.

Let the starry immensities therefore expand into an ever more prodigious repository of assembled suns;

let the light-rays prolong indefinitely, at each end of the spectrum, the range of their hues and their penetrative power;

let life draw from yet more distant sources the sap which flows through its innumerable branches;

and let us go on and on endlessly increasing our perception of the hidden powers that slumber, and the infinitesimally tiny ones that swarm about us, and the immensities that escape us because they appear to us simply as a point.

From all these discoveries, each of which plunges him a little deeper into the ocean of energy, the mystic derives an unalloyed delight, and his thirst for them is unquenchable; for he will never feel himself sufficiently dominated by the powers of the earth and the skies to be brought under God's yoke as completely as he would wish.

It is in fact God, God alone, who through his Spirit stirs up into a ferment the mass of the universe.

PIERRE TEILHARD DE CHARDIN (1881–1955)

I Bind Unto Myself

I bind unto myself today
the virtues of the star-lit heaven,
the glorious sun's life-giving ray,
the whiteness of the moon at even.
The flashing of the lightning free,
the whirling winds' tempestuous shocks,
the stable earth, the deep salt sea
around the old eternal rocks.

SAINT PATRICK (385–461)

Keeping Faith

Keeping Faith

Much of this collection is to do with looking and talking and thinking. There is an old saying in the Bible however that he who listens but does not act is like someone who looks in a mirror and only sees his own face. He becomes narcissistic.

Today the proper stewardship of the earth is a matter of great popular concern although for all the sound and argument over the last ten years, groups like the Nature Conservancy Council can still list a frightening number of habitats lost. Cruelty and exploitation, the maximisation of economic returns for human ends and a commitment to short-term interest is seen as often today as in any age. If anyone speaks of God, faces go blank and conversation shifts to the rights of the badger or the cost of living. Yet if we accept that God gave mankind dominion over all the earth, we must also accept the responsibility of caring for his creation.

The Sixth Day of Creation

Genesis 1 : 26–31

Then God said, "Let us make man in our image, after our
likeness; and let them have dominion over the fish of the sea,
and over the birds of the air, and over the cattle, and over all
the earth, and over every creeping thing that creeps upon the
earth." So God created man in his own image, in the image
of God he created him; male and female he created them. And
God blessed them, and God said to them, "Be fruitful and
multiply, and fill the earth and subdue it; and have dominion
over the fish of the sea and over the birds of the air and over
every living thing that moves upon the earth." And God said,
"Behold, I have given you every plant yielding seed which is
upon the face of all the earth, and every tree with seed in its
fruit; you shall have them for food. And to every beast of the
earth, and to every bird of the air, and to everything that creeps
on the earth, everything that has the breath of life, I have given
every green plant for food." And it was so. And God saw
everything that he had made, and behold, it was very good.
And there was evening and there was morning, a sixth day.

Man Made I

from Paradise Lost

Now heaven in all her glory shone, and roll'd
Her motions, as the great First Mover's hand
First wheel'd their course; earth in her rich attire
Consummate lovely smil'd; air, water, earth,
By fowl, fish, beast, was flown, was swum, was walk'd
Frequent; and of the sixth day yet remain'd;
There wanted yet the master work, the end
Of all yet done; a creature, who not prone
And brute as other creatures, but indu'd
With sanctity of reason, might erect
His stature, and upright with front serene
Govern the rest, self-knowing; and from thence
Magnanimous to correspond with heav'n;
But grateful to acknowledge whence his good
Descends, thither with heart, and voice, and eyes
Directed in devotion, to adore
And worship God supreme, who made him chief
Of all his works: therefore the omnipotent
Eternal Father, for where is not he
Present? thus to his Son audibly spake.
  Let us make now man in our image, man
In our similitude, and let them rule
Over the fish and fowl of sea and air,
Beast of the field, and over all the earth,
And every creeping thing that creeps the ground.

JOHN MILTON (1608–1674)

Man Made II

from The Sword in the Stone

"The asking and granting took up two long days – they were the fifth and sixth, so far as I remember – and at the very end of the sixth day, just before it was time to knock off for Sunday, they had got through all the little embryos except one. This embryo was Man.

" 'Well, Our little man,' said God. 'You have waited till the last, and slept on your decision, and We are sure you have been thinking hard all the time. What can We do for you?'

" 'Please God,' said the embryo, 'I think that You made me in the shape which I now have for reasons best known to Yourselves, and that it would be rude to change. If I am to have my choice I will stay just as I am. I will not alter any of the parts which You gave to me, for other and doubtless inferior tools, and I will stay a defenceless embryo all my life, doing my best to make unto myself a few feeble implements out of the wood, iron and other materials which You have seen fit to put before me. If I want a boat I will endeavour to construct it out of trees, and if I want to fly I will put together a chariot to do it for me. Probably I have been very silly in refusing to take advantage of Your kind offer, but I have done my best to think it over carefully, and now hope that the feeble decision of this small innocent will find favour with Yourselves.'

" 'Well done,' exclaimed the Creator in delighted tones. 'Here, all you embryos, come here with your beaks and what-nots to look upon Our first Man. He is the only one who has guessed Our riddle, out of all of you, and We have great pleasure in conferring upon him the Order of Dominion over the Fowls of the Air, and the Beasts of the Earth, and the Fishes of the Sea. Now let the rest of you get along, and love and multiply, for it is time to knock off for the week-end. As for you, Man, you will be a naked tool all your life, though a user of tools: you will look like an embryo till they bury you, but all others will be embryos before your might; eternally undeveloped, you will always remain *potential* in Our image, able to see some of Our sorrows and to feel some of Our joys. We are partly sorry for you, Man, and partly happy, but always proud. Run along then, Man, and do your best. And listen, Man, before you go . . .'

" 'Well?' asked Adam, turning back from his dismissal.

" 'We were only going to say,' said God shyly, twisting Their hands together. 'Well, We were just going to say, God bless you.' "

T. H. WHITE (1906–1964)

The Making of Narnia

from The Magician's Nephew

The Lion, whose eyes never blinked, stared at the animals as hard as if he was going to burn them up with his mere stare. And gradually a change came over them. The smaller ones – the rabbits, moles and such-like – grew a good deal larger. The very big ones – you noticed it most with the elephants – grew a little smaller. Many animals sat up on their hind legs. Most put their heads on one side as if they were trying hard to understand. The Lion opened his mouth, but no sound came from it; he was breathing out, a long, warm breath; it seemed to sway all the beasts as the wind sways a line of trees. Far overhead from beyond the veil of blue sky which hid them the stars sang again: a pure, cold, difficult music. Then there came a swift flash like fire (but it burnt nobody) either from the sky or from the Lion itself, and every drop of blood tingled in the children's bodies, and the deepest, wildest voice they had ever heard was saying:

"Narnia, Narnia, Narnia, awake. Love. Think. Speak. Be walking trees. Be talking beasts. Be divine waters."

C. S. LEWIS (1898–1963)

Rapid Change in the Natural World

from The Living Planet

The natural world is not static, nor has it ever been. Forests have turned into grassland, savannahs have become deserts, estuaries have silted up and become marshes, ice caps have advanced and retreated. Rapid though these changes have been, seen in the perspective of geological history, animals and plants have been able to respond to them and so maintain a continuity of fertility almost everywhere. But man is now imposing such swift changes that organisms seldom have time to adapt to them. And the scale of our changes is now gigantic. We are so skilled in our engineering, so inventive with chemicals, that we can, in a few months, transform not merely a stretch of a stream or a corner of a wood, but a whole river system, an entire forest.

If we are to manage the world sensibly and effectively we have to decide what our management objectives are. Three international organisations, the International Union for the Conservation of Nature, the United Nations Environmental Programme, and the World Wildlife Fund, have cooperated to do so. They have stated three basic principles that should guide us.

First, we must not exploit natural stocks of animals and plants so intensively that they are unable to renew themselves, and ultimately disappear. This seems such obvious sense that it is hardly worth stating. Yet the anchoveta shoals were fished out in Peru, the herring has been driven away from its old breeding grounds in European waters, and many kinds of whales are still being hunted and are still in real danger of extermination.

Second, we must not so grossly change the face of the earth that we interfere with the basic processes that sustain life – the oxygen content of the atmosphere, the fertility of the seas – and that could happen if we continue destroying the earth's green cover of forests and if we continue using the oceans as a dumping ground for our poisons.

And thirdly, we must do our utmost to maintain the diversity of the earth's animals and plants. It is not just that we depend on many of them for our food – though that is the case. It is not just that we still know so little about them or the practical value they might have for us in the future – though that, too, is so. It is, surely, that we have no moral right to exterminate for ever the creatures with which we share this earth.

As far as we can tell, our planet is the only place in all the black immensities of the universe where life exists. We are alone in space. And the continued existence of life now rests in our hands.

DAVID ATTENBOROUGH (1926–)

Call for a Halt

A world from which solitude is extirpated, is a very poor ideal. Solitude, in the sense of being often alone, is essential to any depth of meditation or of character; and solitude in the presence of natural beauty and grandeur, is the cradle of thoughts and aspirations which are not only good for the individual, but which society could ill do without. Nor is there much satisfaction in contemplating the world with nothing left to the spontaneous activity of nature; with every rood of land brought into cultivation, which is capable of growing food for human beings; every flowery waste or natural pasture ploughed up, all quadrupeds or birds which are not domesticated for man's use exterminated as his rivals for food, every hedgerow or superfluous tree rooted out, and scarcely a place left where a wild shrub or flower could grow without being eradicated as a weed in the name of improved agriculture. If the earth must lose that great portion of its pleasantness which it owes to things that the unlimited increase of wealth and population would extirpate from it, for the mere purpose of enabling it to support a larger, but not a better or a happier population, I sincerely hope, for the sake of posterity, that they will be content to be stationary, long before necessity compels them to it.

JOHN STUART MILL (1806–1873)

A Call for Kindness

from Man and the Natural World

Man's rule, said a mid-seventeenth-century divine, was "subordinate and stewardly, not absolutely to do what he list to do with God's creatures". Cruelty to beasts, agreed Sir Matthew Hale, was "tyranny", "breach of trust" and "injustice". It was true that man was "viceroy of creation", wrote Thomas Tryon. But this rule was

> not absolute or tyrannical, but qualified so as it may most conduce, in the first place to the glory of God; secondly to the real use and benefit of man himself, and not to gratify his fierce and wrathful, or foolish and wanton humour; and thirdly as it best tends to the helping, aiding and assisting those beasts to the obtaining of all the advantages their natures are by the great, beautiful and always beneficent creator made capable of.

This view of man's relationship to animals would have a long life. "We seem to be in the place of God to them," reflected the philosopher David Hartley in 1748, "and we are obliged by the same tenure to be their guardians and benefactors."

KEITH THOMAS

Use or Abuse

from Man and the Natural World

Besides, the Judaeo-Christian inheritance was deeply ambivalent. Side by side with the emphasis on man's right to exploit the inferior species went a distinctive doctrine of human stewardship and responsibility for God's creatures. The English theologians who have been quoted so far tended to disregard those sections of the Old Testament which suggest that man has a duty to act responsibly towards God's creation. They passed quickly over the embarrassing passage in Proverbs 12: 10 which taught that a good man regarded the life of his beast, and the section in Hosea 2: 18 which implied that animals were members of God's covenant. "That this expression is figurative," said an Oxford professor in 1685 in his commentary on Hosea, "cannot be doubted, seeing the things here named are not fit parties for making a covenant." Many learned men of great judgement, therefore, took the passage to be a mere renewal of the league by which animals were subjected to Adam. As for Proverbs, the commentators gratefully quoted St Paul's question in his first Epistle to the Corinthians (9: 9): "Doth God take care for oxen?" – which they took to mean, perhaps wrongly, that he didn't.

KEITH THOMAS

A Question of Judgment

If a man bottlefeeds a cade lamb, watches it grow, is greeted by its pushing weight careering over a field to meet him, then sends it off to the butcher, parcels it into his deep freeze and enjoys eating it for Sunday lunch, he accepts a certain relationship with the created world. If he fattens cockerels and later wrings their necks and sees them with pleasure grace his table and feed his family; same again. If he grows and cuts cabbages, if he milks cows, the list is endless. If he has anything to do with using the wealth of creation for human use, he must reflect upon his place in the created order. I begin with a faith that the order is created.

The verse from Genesis, "Be fruitful and multiply; fill the earth and subdue it, rule over the fish in the sea, the birds of heaven, and every living thing that moves upon the earth." Only the primary producer actually knows what it means to tend and rule and subdue with his own hands. These things remain book learning for the townsman, bright ideas untarnished, unenriched by the necessity to kill as well as to bring to birth. That necessity of the primary producer does something to mature his judgement; can do something if he reflects. The young are often unthinking; constant labour makes for calluses; not everyone sees God as creator and enjoys the lively beauty of his world. But enough do.

> The innocent brightness of the new born day is lovely yet
> The clouds that gather round the setting sun
> Do take a sober colouring from an eye
> That hath kept watch on man's mortality.

And so it is to a lesser extent with the death of brother lamb and brother cockerel. A farmer may well speak with genuine affection of his lambs. "Come my little ones." Even that ancient shepherd, Polyphemus, spoke affectionately to his ram, "Oh my pet ram, why are you last out of the cave for me?"

But neither Polyphemus nor the farmer today would think of setting up a hospital for ageing rams and ewes.

And so the fruit farmer kills the aphis and the larva of the codling moth. The gardener does his best to destroy the hosts of the scale insects and the potato-boring wireworm and the leaf-killing red spider. Thorn hedges are cut and laid to keep in livestock. Trees are felled for the carpenter and for firewood. The ground is scarred for building materials. The gardener plants shrubs close together; one he must uproot if the other is to thrive.

MERVYN WILSON (1933–)

Wanton Pastimes

from Ethics

Whenever I injure life of any kind I must be quite clear as to whether this is necessary or not. I ought never to pass the limits of the unavoidable, even in apparently insignificant cases. The countryman who has mowed down a thousand blossoms in his meadow as fodder for his cows should take care that on the way home he does not, in wanton pastime, switch off the head of a single flower growing on the edge of the road, for in so doing he injures life without being forced to do so by necessity.

ALBERT SCHWEITZER (1875–1965)

Cruelty

A Robin Red breast in a Cage
Puts all Heaven in a Rage.
A dove house fill'd with doves & Pigeons
Shudders Hell thro' all its regions.
A dog starv'd at his Master's Gate
Predicts the ruin of the State.
A Horse misus'd upon the Road
Calls to Heaven for Human blood.
Each outcry of the hunted Hare
A fibre from the Brain does tear.
A Skylark wounded in the wing,
A Cherubim does cease to sing.
The Game Cock clip'd & arm'd for fight
Does the Rising Sun affright.
Every Wolf's & Lion's howl
Raises from Hell a Human Soul.
The wild deer, wand'ring here & there,
Keeps the Human Soul from Care.
The Lamb misus'd breeds Public strife
And yet forgives the Butcher's Knife.
The Bat that flits at close of Eve
Has left the Brain that won't Believe.
The Owl that calls upon the Night
Speaks the Unbeliever's fright.
He who shall hurt the little Wren
Shall never be belov'd by Men.
He who the Ox to wrath has mov'd
Shall never be by Woman lov'd.
The wanton Boy that kills the Fly
Shall feel the Spider's enmity.
He who torments the Chafer's sprite
Weaves a Bower in endless Night.
The Caterpillar on the Leaf

Repeats to thee thy Mother's grief.
Kill not the Moth nor Butterfly,
For the Last Judgment draweth nigh.

WILLIAM BLAKE (1757–1827)

A Trust Betrayed

from Cry the Beloved Country

There is a lovely road that runs from Ixopo into the hills. These hills are grass-covered and rolling, and they are lovely beyond any singing of it. The road climbs seven miles into them, to Carisbrooke; and from there, if there is no mist, you look down on one of the fairest valleys of Africa. About you there is grass and bracken and you may hear the forlorn crying of the titihoya, one of the birds of the veld. Below you is the valley of the Umzimkulu, on its journey from the Drakensberg to the sea; and beyond and behind the river, great hill after great hill; and beyond and behind them, the mountains of Ingeli and East Griqualand.

The grass is rich and matted, you cannot see the soil. It holds the rain and the mist, and they seep into the ground, feeding the streams in every kloof. It is well-tended, and not too many cattle feed upon it; not too many fires burn it, laying bare the soil. Stand unshod upon it, for the ground is holy, being even as it came from the Creator. Keep it, guard it, care for it, for it keeps men, guards men, cares for men. Destroy it and man is destroyed.

Where you stand the grass is rich and matted, you cannot see the soil. But the rich green hills break down. They fall to the valley below, and falling, change their nature. For they grow red and bare; they cannot hold the rain and mist, and the streams are dry in the kloofs. Too many cattle feed upon the grass, and too many fires have burned it. Stand shod upon it, for it is coarse and sharp, and the stones cut under the feet. It is not kept, or guarded, or cared for, it no longer keeps men, guards men, cares for men. The titihoya does not cry here any more.

ALAN PATON (1903–1988)

Creation Betrayed

Hosea 4: 1–4

There is no good faith or mutal trust,
no knowledge of God in the land,
oaths are imposed and broken, they kill and rob;
there is nothing but adultery and licence,
one deed of blood after another.
Therefore the land shall be dried up,
and all who live in it shall pine away,
and with them the wild beasts and the birds of the air;
even the fish shall be swept from the sea.
But it is not for any man to bring a charge,
it is not for him to prove a case;
the quarrel with you, false priest, is mine.

If a Man Keep Faith

Psalm 107: 31–41

O that men would therefore praise the Lord for his goodness: and declare the wonders that he doeth for the children of men!

That they would exalt him also in the congregation of the people: and praise him in the seat of the elders!

Who turneth the floods into a wilderness: and drieth up the water-springs.

A fruitful land maketh he barren: for the wickedness of them that dwell therein.

Again, he maketh the wilderness a standing water: and water-springs of a dry ground.

And there he setteth the hungry: that they may build them a city to dwell in;

That they may sow their land, and plant vineyards: to yield them fruits of increase.

He blesseth them, so that they multiply exceedingly: and suffereth not their cattle to decrease.

And again, when they are minished, and brought low: through oppression, through any plague, or trouble;

Though he suffer them to be evil intreated through tyrants: and let them wander out of the way in the wilderness;

Yet helpeth he the poor out of misery: and maketh him households like a flock of sheep.

The Difficult Land

This is a difficult land. Here things miscarry
Whether we care, or do not care enough.
The grain may pine, the harlot weed grow haughty,
Sun, rain, and frost alike conspire against us:
You'd think there was malice in the very air.
And the spring floods and summer droughts: our fields
Mile after mile of soft and useless dust.
On dull delusive days presaging rain
We yoke the oxen, go out harrowing,
Walk in the middle of an ochre cloud,
Dust rising before us and falling again behind us,
Slowly and gently settling where it lay.
These days the earth itself looks sad and senseless.
And when next day the sun mounts hot and lusty
We shake our fists and kick the ground in anger.
We have strange dreams: as that, in the early morning
We stand and watch the silver drift of stars
Turn suddenly to a flock of black-birds flying.
And once in a life-time men from over the border,
In early summer, the season of fresh campaigns,
Come trampling down the corn, and kill our cattle.
These things we know and by good luck or guidance
Either frustrate or, if we must, endure.
We are a people; race and speech support us,
Ancestral rite and custom, roof and tree,
Our songs that tell of our triumphs and disasters
(Fleeting alike), continuance of fold and hearth,
Our names and callings, work and rest and sleep,
And something that, defeated, still endures –
These things sustain us. Yet there are times
When name, identity, and our very hands,
Senselessly labouring, grow most hateful to us,
And we would gladly rid us of these burdens
(Which yet are knit to us as flesh to bone),

Enter our darkness through the doors of wheat
And the light veil of grass (leaving behind
Name, body, country, speech, vocation, faith)
And gather into the secrecy of the earth
Furrowed by broken ploughs lost deep in time.

We have such hours, but are drawn back again
By faces of goodness, faithful masks of sorrow,
Honesty, kindness, courage, fidelity,
The love that lasts a life's time. And the fields,
Homestead and stall and barn, springtime and autumn.
(For we can love even the wandering seasons
In their inhuman circuit.) And the dead
Who lodge in us so strangely, unremembered,
Yet in their place. For how can we reject
The long last look on the ever-dying face
Turned backward from the other side of time?
And how offend the dead and shame the living
By these despairs? And how refrain from love?
This is a difficult country, and our home.

EDWIN MUIR (1887–1958)

Living in Peace

from Christianity and the Rights of Animals

We return in this way to our opening remarks concerning the need for humility as well as vision. What we need is *progressive* disengagement from our inhumanity to animals. The urgent and essential task is to invite, encourage, support and welcome those who want to take some steps along the road to a more peaceful world with the non-human creation. We do not *all* have to agree upon the most vital steps, or indeed the most practical ones.

What is important is that we all move some way on, if only by one step at a time, however falteringly. To my mind every pheasant which is left to live rather than shot is a gain. If that is all the humanity one hunter can muster at least we have saved one creature. If we can encourage one researcher to save one mouse, at least that is one mouse saved. If we can persuade an intensive farmer to refrain from de-beaking one hen then at least some small burden of suffering is lessened in the world. The enemy of progress is the view that everything must be changed before some real gains can be secured. Some may disagree with the major contours as well as the details of the vision I have outlined. Some may argue that such and such a judgement is too hard or such and such an option is too soft. There can be areas of genuine disagreement even among those who are committed to a new world of animal rights. But what is essential for this new world to emerge is the sense that each of us can change our individual worlds, however slightly, to live more peaceably with our non-human neighbours.

"I could not but feel with a sympathy full of regret all the pain that I saw around me, not only that of men, but that of the whole creation," wrote Schweitzer in a telling passage in his autobiography. "From this community of suffering, I have never tried to withdraw myself." He concluded: "It seemed to me a matter of course that we should all take our share of the burden of suffering which lies upon the world. The vision of Christ-like lordship over the non-human is practically costly. Our moral choices inevitably entail sacrifice and pain. In this way we anticipate, if not actually realize, the future joy of all God's creatures.

ANDREW LINZEY (1952–)

Balaam's Ass Speaks

Numbers 22: 21–35

So Balaam rose in the morning, and saddled his ass, and went with the princes of Moab. But God's anger was kindled because he went; and the angel of the LORD took his stand in the way as his adversary. Now he was riding on the ass, and his two servants were with him.

And the ass saw the angel of the Lord standing in the road, with a drawn sword in his hand; and the ass turned aside out of the road, and went into the field; and Balaam struck the ass, to turn her into the road. Then the angel of the LORD stood in a narrow path between the vineyards, with a wall on either side.

And when the ass saw the angel of the LORD, she pushed against the wall, and pressed Balaam's foot against the wall; so he struck her again. Then the angel of the LORD went ahead, and stood in a narrow place, where there was no way to turn either to the right or to the left. When the ass saw the angel of the LORD, she lay down under Balaam; and Balaam's anger was kindled, and he struck the ass with his staff.

Then the LORD opened the mouth of the ass, and she said to Balaam, "What have I done to you, that you have struck me these three times?" And Balaam said to the ass, "Because you have made sport of me. I wish I had a sword in my hand, for then I would kill you." And the ass said to Balaam, "Am I not your ass, upon which you have ridden all your life long to this day? Was I ever accustomed to do so to you?" And he said, "No."

Then the LORD opened the eyes of Balaam, and he saw the angel of the LORD standing in the way, with his drawn sword in his hand; and he bowed his head, and fell on his face. And the angel of the LORD said to him, "Why have you struck your ass three times? Behold, I have come forth to withstand you, because your way is perverse before me; and the ass saw me,

192

and turned aside before me these three times. If she had not turned aside from me, surely just now I would have slain you and let her live." Then Balaam said to the angel of the LORD, "I have sinned, for I did not know that thou didst stand in the road against me. Now therefore, if it is evil in thy sight, I will go back again." And the angel of the LORD said to Balaam, "Go with the men; but only the word which I bid you, that shall you speak." So Balaam went on with the princes of Balak.

The Talking Horse

from The Horse and His Boy

"In other words," it continued, "you *can't* ride. That's a drawback. I'll have to teach you as we go along. If you can't ride, can you fall?"

"I suppose anyone can fall," said Shasta.

"I mean can you fall and get up again without crying and mount again and fall again and yet not be afraid of falling?"

"I – I'll try," said Shasta.

"Poor little beast," said the Horse in a gentler tone. "I forget you're only a foal. We'll make a fine rider of you in time. And now – we mustn't start until those two in the hut are asleep. Meantime we can make our plans. My Tarkaan is on his way North to the great city, to Tashbaan itself and the court of the Tisroc – "

"I say," put in Shasta in rather a shocked voice, "oughtn't you to say "May he live for ever?" "

"Why?" asked the Horse. "I'm a free Narnian. And why should I talk slaves' and fools' talk? I don't want him to live for ever, and I know that he's not going to live for ever whether I want him to or not. And I can see you're from the free North too."

C. S. LEWIS (1898–1963)

Sympathy with Animals

Man comes again and again into the position of being able to preserve his own life and life generally only at the cost of other life. If he has been touched by the ethic of reverence for life, he injures and destroys life only under a necessity which he cannot avoid and never from thoughtlessness. So far as he is a free man he uses every opportunity of tasting the blessedness of being able to assist life and avert from it suffering and destruction.

Devoted as I was from boyhood to the cause of the protection of animal life, it is a special joy to me that the universal ethic of reverence for life shows the sympathy with animals which is so often represented as sentimentality, to be a duty which no thinking man can escape. Hitherto ethics have faced the problem of man and beast either uncomprehending or helpless. Even when sympathy with the animal creation was felt to be right, it could not be brought within the scope of ethics, because ethics were really focused only on the behaviour of man to man.

ALBERT SCHWEITZER (1875–1965)

Land,
Work and Character

Land, Work and Character

The Japanese have a saying that if you want to grow to a happy and healthy old age then take up thinking and gardening. Others from the earliest times have held that manual work for a moderate reward was good for the nation as well as for the individual.

The *Rule of Saint Benedict*, so influential in Western Europe, lays down a balance of prayer, learning, charitable activity and work with the hands. The many thousands of monks who lived by this Rule changed the face of Europe in their day and left us an example worth following.

Here are gathered together pieces about working on the land. No substitute for the real thing, but maybe an incentive to try it.

How Can They Live in God's Way?

from Winding Quest

Farmer
  ploughing the field, proud of his goad,
  driving his oxen, lost to the world,
  talking, talking of cattle,
  following the furrow by day,
  fattening the heifers by night?

Blacksmith
  sitting by his anvil in a world of pig-iron,
  scorched by the forge, fighting the furnace heat,
  deafened by hammers' din, rapt in his pattern,
  firm to finish his work, fashioning it into the night?

Potter
  working at his wheel, turning it with his feet,
  lost in his task of making up his tally,
  slapping and puddling the clay,
  engrossed in his glazing,
  staying awake cleaning out his kiln?

These men trust their hands;
  their craftsmanship is their wisdom.
Without them cities would be empty –
  nobody living there,
  nobody coming and going.
You won't hear them in the City Council
  or see them sitting in the Assembly;
you won't find them among the judges –

they can't make head or tail of the Law;
they don't talk like scholars –
  they can't quote the critics.
Yet they hold the world in their hands;
  their worship is in their work.

Ecclesiasticus 38 tr. ALAN DALE

The Good Farmer

from Works and Days

O noble Perses, keep my words in mind,
And work till Hunger is your enemy
And till Demeter, awesome, garlanded,
Becomes your friend and fills your granary.
For Hunger always loves a lazy man;
Both gods and men despise him, for he is
Much like the stingless drone, who does not work
But eats, and wastes the effort of the bees.
But you must learn to organize your work
So you may have full barns at harvest time.
From working, men grow rich in flocks and gold
And dearer to the deathless gods. In work
There is no shame; shame is in idleness
And if you work, the lazy man will soon
Envy your wealth: a rich man can become
Famous and good. No matter what your luck,
To work is better; turn your foolish mind
From other men's possessions to your own,
And earn your living, as I tell you to.
A cringing humbleness accompanies
The needy man, a humbleness which may
Destroy or profit him. The humble are
The poor men, while the rich are self-assured.
Money should not be seized; that gold which is
God's gift is better. If a man gets wealth
By force of hands or through his lying tongue,
As often happens, when greed clouds his mind
And shame is pushed aside by shamelessness,
Then the gods blot him out and blast his house
And soon his wealth deserts him. Also, he
Who harms a guest or suppliant, or acts
Unseemly, sleeping with his brother's wife,

Or in his folly, hurts an orphan child,
Or he who picks rough quarrels, and attacks
His father at the threshold of old age,
He angers Zeus himself, and in the end
He pays harsh penalties for all his sins.

HESIOD (8th century B.C.)

Good Practice

Ecclesiastes 11: 4–6

He who watches the wind will never sow, and he who keeps an eye on the clouds will never reap. You do not know how a pregnant woman comes to have a body and a living spirit in her womb; nor do you know how God, the maker of all things, works. In the morning sow your seed betimes, and do not stop work until evening, for you do not know whether this or that sowing will be successful, or whether both alike will do well.

The Happy Farmer

from Georgics

How lucky, if they know their happiness,
Are farmers, more than lucky, they for whom,
Far from the clash of arms, the earth herself,
Most fair in dealing, freely lavishes
An easy livelihood. What if no palace
With arrogant portal out of every cranny
Belches a mighty tide of morning callers
And no one gapes at doors inlaid so proudly
With varied tortoiseshell, cloth tricked with gold
And rare Corinthian bronzes? What if wool
Is white, not tainted with Assyrian poison,
And honest olive oil not spoilt with cassia?
Yet peace they have and a life of innocence
Rich in variety; they have for leisure
Their ample acres, caverns, living lakes,
Cool Temples; cattle low, and sleep is soft
Under a tree. Coverts of game are there
And glades, a breed of youth inured to labour
And undemanding, worship of the gods
And reverence for the old. Departing Justice
Left among these her latest earthly footprints.

VIRGIL (70–19 B.C.)

A Waste Made to Flower

from Georgics

I well remember how, beneath the towers
Of old Tarentum where the dark Galaesus
Waters the yellow crops, I saw a man,
An old Cilician, who occupied
And acre or two of land that no one wanted,
A patch not worth the ploughing, unrewarding
For flocks, unfit for vineyards; he however
By planting here and there among the scrub
Cabbages or white lilies and verbena
And flimsy poppies, fancied himself a king
In wealth, and coming home late in the evening
Loaded his board with unbought delicacies.
He was the first in spring to gather roses,
In autumn, to pick apples; and when winter
Was gloomily still cracking rocks with cold
And choking streams with ice, he was already
Shearing the locks of the tender hyacinth
While grumbling at the lateness of the summer
And absence of west winds. And his again
Were the first bees to breed, the first to swarm
Abundantly and have their foaming honey
Squeezed from the combs. Plenty of limes he had
And laurustinus; and all the fruit a tree
Promised in blossom-time's array to bear
It bore matured in autumn. Elms well-grown,
Pear-trees already hardened, even blackthorns
Already bearing sloes and planes already
Providing welcome shade for drinking parties
He planted out in rows successfully.

VIRGIL (70–19 B.C.)

God's Farm

God, whose farm is all creation,
   take the gratitude we give;
take the finest of our harvest,
   crops we grow that men may live.

Take our ploughing, seeding, reaping,
   hopes and fears of sun and rain,
all our thinking, planning, waiting,
   ripened in this fruit and grain.

All our labour, all our watching,
   all our calendar of care,
in these crops of your creation,
   take, O God: they are our prayer.

JOHN ARLOTT (1914–)

New Thinking

from Rushall: The Story of an Organic Farm

Once you start thinking along these lines – the way chemicals affect ecological chains, setting up potentially destructive chain reactions, and the safety procedures regulating the introduction of new chemicals – you cannot help becoming more and more worried at the practices of modern agriculture. Remember, these thoughts were going through my head in the 1960s – now many more people are realizing that we may well be headed for catastrophe – and it was at that time that I decided that I would see whether it was possible to farm organically. To be fair, we at Rushall were in the fortunate position of having a lot of land, due, as I have said, to the foresight of my father and grandfather, and so we could afford to experiment. This work, I maintain, should have been undertaken by the Ministry of Agriculture, either by devoting one of its experimental husbandry farms to research into organic methods, or by conducting the same research on parts of all its farms. In spite of repeated efforts on my part, and latterly by the organic movement generally, the Ministry has never faced up to the challenge. One day it will regret this.

I leave the last word with Frederick W. H. Myers (1843–1901):

Dreamers of dreams? We take the taunt with gladness
Knowing that God, beyond the years we see,
Has brought the dreams that count with man for madness
Into the fabric of the world to be.

BARRY WOOKEY

Old Work

from The English Countryman

At first sight, it might appear that the claim for Hodge the husbandman as the painter of the English landscape – and be it remembered that if God made the hills, it was Hodge's sheep that turfed them, Hodge's burial mounds and stone circles that focused their grandeur and Hodge's stone walls that ribbed and articulated them – were somewhat compromised by Mr Bell's richly toned etching of the Fens. Mr Bell describes a purely man-made landscape whose intensive cultivation is intermixed with mechanical device that extends into the country the methods of urbanised mass-production. Cultivation there is a business rather than a craft, and business and craftsmanship are to my mind fundamentally incompatible. It was the importation of the commercial idea into the countryside of the Tudor graziers in the sixteenth century that submitted the crafts and so the country and so the landscape to a process of slow strangulation. The fruits of that grafting set our teeth on edge to-day.

There are two very good reasons why a *living* countryside can never be mechanised except at the expense in the end both of the landscape and the life. Apart from the contradiction in terms between life and mechanism, an industrialised country-side no longer depends upon itself but upon a financial system whose node is the city. If it breaks down, the country reverts and ceases to be the landscape patiently modelled by millenia of husbandry. Secondly, a man-modified Nature (which is what English country is) has been built upon growing things, that is to say, upon bread and cheese, on the basis, that is to say, of utility. Now utility is the be-all if it is not the end-all of craftsmanship and craftsmanship can never be properly understood unless it be realised that its beauty comes last because its utility comes first. When the masons were building Ely Cathedral (which is to the Fens in terms of landscape what the sun is to the sky), they were considering problems of structure, or how best to praise God in terms of stone which should interpret what they knew of the laws of Nature and the universe. Nature, too, considers utility in terms of life and that is why the craftsman can be seen all through the ages to fit so marvellously into Nature, until he makes a countryside that is a third entity fusing the qualities of them both.

H. J. MASSINGHAM (1888–1952)

Old Piety

from The English Countryman

But the faithful round proceeds as the faithful seasons pass and in the autumn Giles looses the pigs among the oaks that, meeting the mallard startled from her pool:

> "decamp with more than swinish speed,
> And snorting dash through sedge and rush and reed:
> Through tangling thickets headlong on they go,
> Then stop and listen for their fancied foe."

The comfort of Nature is still with the humiliated and the dispossessed, and her shrillest or iciest mood is not the spiritual wound the farmer gives not merely by his sweating wage but the new social cleavage between him and his men.

Through all the defects of the labourer poets, we perceive the husbandly faith still intact from peasant times, the old piety of the labour of the fields. Even in our age it is still with us, though the modern farmers strive to turn farm into firm and the local authority has deprived the labourer of the last item of his peasant property – his pig. Arthur Young in his conversion from Saul to Paul understood the importance of the pig to the cottager and in nothing is the divorce between country and town more clearly exposed than in the urban fantasy that cheap and easy access to the cinema is to the countryman a compensation for the loss of his pigsty. The rational planners who pour out pamphlets about the new England to be fail to realize it and so the variety and interest of a normal country life and so the profound meaning of the little man's private property.

H. J. MASSINGHAM (1888–1952)

The Serf

His naked skin clothed in the torrid mist
   That puffs in smoke around the patient hooves,
The ploughman drives, a slow somnambulist,
   And through the green his crimson furrow grooves.
His heart, more deeply than he wounds the plain,
   Long by the rasping share of insult torn,
Red clod, to which the war-cry once was rain
   And tribal spears the fatal sheaves of corn,
Lies fallow now. But as the turf divides
I see in the slow progress of his strides
   Over the toppled clods and falling flowers,
The timeless, surly patience of the serf
That moves the nearest to the naked earth
   And ploughs down palaces, and thrones, and towers.

ROY CAMPBELL (1901–1957)

Ploughing the Sea

from Mirror of the Sea

Yes; it needed a few days after the taking of your departure for a ship's company to shake down into their places, and for the soothing deep-water ship routine to establish its beneficent sway.

It is a great doctor for sore hearts and sore heads, too, your ship's routine, which I have seen soothe – at least for a time – the most turbulent of spirits. There is health in it, and peace, and satisfaction of the accomplished round; for each day of the ship's life seems to close a circle within the wide ring of the sea horizon. It borrows a certain dignity of sameness from the majestic monotony of the sea. He who loves the sea loves also the ship's routine.

Nowhere else than upon the sea do the days, weeks, and months fall away quicker into the past. They seem to be left astern as easily as the light air-bubbles in the swirls of the ship's wake, and vanish into a great silence in which your ship moves on with a sort of magical effect. They pass away, the days, the weeks, the months. Nothing but a gale can disturb the orderly life of the ship; and the spell of unshaken monotony that seems to have fallen upon the very voices of her men is broken only by the near prospect of a Landfall.

JOSEPH CONRAD (1857–1924)

The Ploughman

from The Everlasting Mercy

Up the slow slope a team came bowing,
Old Callow at his autumn ploughing,
Old Callow, stooped above the hales,
Ploughing the stubble into wales;
His grave eyes looking straight ahead,
Shearing a long straight furrow red;
His plough-foot high to give it earth
To bring new food for men to birth . . .

O Christ who holds the open gate,
O Christ who drives the furrow straight,

O Christ, the plough, O Christ, the laughter
Of holy white birds flying after,
Lo, all my heart's field red and torn,
And Thou wilt bring the young green corn,
The young green corn divinely springing,
The young green corn for ever singing;
And when the field is fresh and fair
Thy blessèd feet shall glitter there.
And we will walk the weeded field,
And tell the golden harvest's yield,
The corn that makes the holy bread
By which the soul of man is fed,
The holy bread, the food unpriced,
Thy everlasting mercy, Christ.

The share will jar on many a stone,
Thou wilt not let me stand alone;
And I shall feel (Thou wilt not fail),
Thy hand on mine upon the hale . . .

I crossed the hedge by Shooter's Gap,
I hitched my boxer's belt a strap,
I jumped the ditch and crossed the fallow,
I took the hales from farmer Callow.

JOHN MASEFIELD (1878–1967)

Singing at Work

from Lark Rise to Candleford

Most of the men sang or whistled as they dug or hoed. There was a good deal of outdoor singing in those days. Workmen sang at their jobs; men with horses and carts sang on the road; the baker, the miller's man, and the fish-hawker sang as they went from door to door; even the doctor and parson on their rounds hummed a tune between their teeth. People were poorer and had not the comforts, amusements, or knowledge we have today; but they were happier. Which seems to suggest that happiness depends more upon the state of mind – and body, perhaps – than upon circumstances and events.

FLORA THOMPSON (1876–1947)

Tools

from A Gardening Credo

There is a lovable quality about the actual tools. One feels so kindly to the thing that enables the hand to obey the brain. Moreover, one feels a good deal of respect for it; without it brain and hand would be helpless. When the knife that has been in one's hand or one's pocket for years has its blade so much worn by constant sharpening that it can no longer be used, with what true regret does one put it aside, and how long it is before one can really make friends with the new one! I do not think any workman really likes a new tool. There is always some feeling about it as of something strange and unfamiliar and uncongenial, somewhat of the feeling that David had about Saul's armour. What an awkward thing a new spade is, how long and heavy and rough of handle! And then how amiable it becomes when it is half worn, when the square corners that made the thrust so hard are ground away, when the whole blade has grown shorter, when the handle has gained that polish, the best polish of all, that comes of long hand-friction. No carpenter likes a new plane; no house-painter likes a new brush. It is the same with tools as with clothes.

GERTRUDE JEKYLL (1843–1932)

Work

from A Gardening Credo

If it were possible to simplify life to the utmost, how little one really wants! And is it a blessing or a disadvantage to be so made that one must take keen interest in many matters; that, seeing something that one's hands may do, one cannot resist doing or attempting it, even though time be already over-crowded, and strength much reduced, and sight steadily failing? Are the people happier who are content to drift comfortably down the stream of life, to take things easily, not to *want* to take pains or give themselves trouble about what is not exactly necessary? I know not which, as wordly wisdom, is the wiser; I only know that to my own mind and conscience pure idleness seems to me to be akin to folly, or even worse, and that in some form or other I must obey the Divine command: "Work while ye have the light."

GERTRUDE JEKYLL (1843–1932)

The Tumbril

from The Cherry Tree

Upon the front of the buck of the tumbril my name went up in a gentle wave, and the address of Silver Ley Farm met it at the crest and led down sinuously across the other side. Above and below and around were gentle flourishes as though the painter had been trying the grace of his curves before beginning, which had miraculously formed a symmetry of soft contours through which the writing meandered like a river. But more; each flourish, thickening in the middle and tailing away, had a grey shadow of itself beside, as though beneath it. As I examined the tumbril I found that edging its square strength were innumerable small decorations, apt as the flower in a yokel's cap – the corner beams were fretted with scallops, and each scallop painted red in contrast to the green of the buck, and there were linings of red here and there, and other evidences of the rough-hewing of its beginning graduating into final moments of exquisite precision. Few indeed, in our days of "fitness for purpose," grow such signs of fancy playing about the feet of toil, the same that led our ancestor to carve his beams and emboss his house-front with a plaster vine.

In edging his most prosaic handiwork with those touches of toy-like decoration, the local craftsman shows himself true to his nature as a reflection of the earth's. I found in it a power of co-ordination, unconscious very likely, as the tumbril toiled loaded over the stubble-field. For pimpernel and late poppy made gay the stark ground even as in spring its bare harrowed earth was edged with oxlips all round the hedge. Such minutiae of beauty ever compensate the huge uncouthness of husbandry, whose rough shoulder is continually rubbing them. As for the stiff coat of the working man, one day it is snow upon its lapels and another blossoms, and the stolid purpose pushes on through all. Thus is man in his first and ultimate environment. A balance of the coarse and fine may be dimly apprehended here, which grows into a nobility hard to define the more it is observed.

ADRIAN BELL (1902–1980)

Mr Webb

I shall never forget a visit to that nursery [Calcot, near Reading] some six-and-twenty years ago. It was walled all round, and a deep-sounding bell had to be rung many times before any one came to open the gate; but at last it was opened by a fine, strongly-built, sunburnt woman of the type of the good working farmer's wife, that I remember as a child. She was the forewoman, who worked the nursery with suprisingly few hands – only three men, if I remember rightly – but she looked as if she could do the work of "all two men" herself. One of the specialties of the place was a fine breed of mastiffs; another was an old Black Hamburg vine, that rambled and clambered in and out of some very old greenhouses, and was wonderfully productive. There were alleys of nuts in all directions, and large spreading patches of palest yellow Daffodils – the double *Narcissus cernuus*, now so scarce and difficult to grow. Had I then known how precious a thing was there in fair abundance, I should not have been contented with the modest dozen that I asked for. It was a most pleasant garden to wander in, especially with the old Mr Webb who presently appeared. He was dressed in black clothes of an old-looking cut – a Quaker, I believe. Never shall I forget an apple-tart he invited me to try as a proof of the merit of the "Wellington" apple. It was not only good, but beautiful; the cooked apple looking rosy and transparent, and most inviting. He told me he was an ardent preacher of total abstinence, and took me to a grassy, shady place among the nuts, where there was an upright stone slab, like a tombstone, with the inscription:

TO ALCOHOL

He had dug a grave, and poured into it a quantity of wine and beer and spirits, and placed the stone as a memorial of his abhorrence of drink. The whole thing remains in my mind like a picture – the shady groves of old nuts, in tenderest early leaf, the pale Daffodils, the mighty chained mastiffs with bloodshot eyes and murderous fangs, the brawny, wholesome forewoman, and the trim old gentleman in black. It was the only nursery I ever saw where one would expect to see fairies on a summer's night.

GERTRUDE JEKYLL (1843–1932)

A Green and Pleasant Land

from The Times, 8 Nov 1983

I have three children and they will, I suppose, have to earn their own living sometime as the year 2000 looms into view. What on earth will they do? If you believe like myself that we will not have eradicated massive, permanent unemployment by then, you will wonder what we can do to find more niches for people who want to work for a living.

Like most people, I imagine that the future will provide something for people prepared to enter into an unholy alliance with machines, such as bankers and accountants, blinking at their VDU's.

But suppose my children – or others – are not born engineers or entrepreneurs? Suppose they are the sort of mild-mannered, hard-working, skilful people who would like a stable sort of a job to do, in which they could display quiet dedication to a job well done?

Nothing made, no job performed, by such people will be able to compete on price with the high-tech product churned out mechanically. Luddites will turn out to have been right all along.

I propose the creation of the New Peasant. Ever since Cobbett saw so clearly that the British middle and upper classes were up to no good when they crushed the peasants we have had cause to mourn the peculiar way in which the decencies of the feudal system were swept away along with its indecencies. We fell prey, he saw, to the world in which the relations of employer and employee were mediated entirely by wages and each was discharged of obligation to the other.

Besides cooperatives, in which people group together to share risk and profit, why shouldn't we discover a new, proper relationship between the owner of capital or land, and the worker who makes something of them?

Several sorts of business would make a good example, one

of them hinted at by John May's letter to *The Times* (September 12). Good forestry is only marginally profitable these days: the better the forestry the less immediately profitable it is. Coppicing, the ancient craft of cropping a woodland so that it produced everything from broom handles to building timber, could allow wood products to compete with plastic and concrete, but only if the taxman, the landowner and the worker all came to a new understanding.

They would all be getting something worthwhile. The state would be helped with foreign exchange by cutting down on imports of oil for the manufacture of plastics; the landowner would have beautiful, rather, than a presently derelict, woodlands, and the worker – the New Peasant – could be given an agreeable, easy going living.

Farming is also ripe for the New Peasant in an age when jobs are increasingly scrapped in favour of petrochemicals.

Intelligent farmers may well be able to strike deals with people offering cheap labour in return for a return to the land and time of their own. It is important to note that the New Peasant is a voluntary peasant, embracing a poverty of cash in exchange for a richness of lifestyle; in a contract in which no subservience was implied.

Water transport offers another opportunity. Energy-efficient inland, coastal or international cargo-carrying is not often profitable (though the sums will increasingly go in their favour as fuel prices rise). The difficulty has been that many transport methods which forgo speed and energy add more to labour costs than they save in fuel cost. But the New Peasant could volunteer to forgo some wages in exchange for working a sailing or canal barge, or a clipper, rather than roaring about in a juggernaut, or whiling away time in tedious supertankers (which already have difficulty in keeping their crews).

The equation of fuel versus labour costs might alter dramatically if the interesting possibility of a slow, fuel-saving sailing ship was run by people who preferred it to the better-paying, rapid, energy-profligate motor vessel.

The New Peasant is a little like the craftsman of the William

Morris movement. Modern craftsmen have in general been dependent for their workshop paradise upon the rich world buying their product at vast expense. Nothing wrong in that, of course. But the New Craftsman should be producing quite ordinary things (foods and services) at ordinary prices. It is this new relationship to the capital and land which imaginative entrepreneurs and workers will have to invent for the next century.

RICHARD NORTH

Times go by Turns

The lopped tree in time may grow again,
  Most naked plants renew both fruit and flower;
The sorriest wight may find release of pain,
  The driest soil suck in some moistening shower.
    Times go by turns, and chances change by course,
    From foul to fair, from better hap to worse.

The sea of Fortune doth not ever flow,
  She draws her favours to the lowest ebb;
Her tides hath equal times to come and go,
  Her loom doth weave the fine and coarsest web.
    No joy so great but runneth to an end,
    No hap so hard but may in fine amend.

Not always fall of leaf, nor ever spring,
  No endless night, yet not eternal day;
The saddest birds a season find to sing,
  The roughest storm a calm may soon allay.
    Thus, with succeeding turns, God tempereth all,
    That man may hope to rise, yet fear to fall.

A chance may win that by mischance was lost;
  The net, that holds no great, takes little fish;
In some things all, in all things none are crossed;
  Few all they need, but none have all they wish.
    Unmeddled joys here to no man befall;
    Who least, hath some; who most, hath never all.

ROBERT SOUTHWELL (1561–1595)

Engagement in Agriculture

The truth is, the portion of lands which belonged to the city of Rome at the beginning, was very narrow; but Romulus by war greatly enlarged it. All this land Numa divided amongst the indigent part of the citizens, that by this means he might keep them from extreme want, which is the necessary cause of mens injuring one another, and might turn the minds of the people to husbandry, whereby themselves as well as their land would become better cultivated and more tractable. For there is no way of life that either so soon or so powerfully produces the love of peace, as the prosession of husbandry, whereby so much courage is preserved as enables men to fight in defence of their own, but that violence and impetuosity which breaks out in acts of injustice and encroachment upon others is checked and restrained. Wherefore Numa engaged his citizens in agriculture as the surest means to make them in love with peace, and chose it for them as an employment fitted rather to improve the temper, than to procure great riches.

PLUTARCH (?46–?120)

Small Dividends

from New Sermons to Asses

In all nations where there is a landed interest, the security of the commonwealth is best maintained by making small and numerous dividends; for thereby the greater number will be interested in the welfare of a nation. But when only a few have a real interest and property in a country, the nerves of government must be considerably weakened. The idea of men labouring for themselves, though it appears selfish, yet will have a greater influence upon their care and diligence, than when they consider themselves toiling principally for the interest of others, who will employ them no longer than they are fit for their service. It is either possession of property, or the hopes thereof, which make men settle in one country more than another; for it is not natural for mankind to reside where they have neither hopes nor possessions, and have nothing before their eyes, except to be slaves or vassals, and to be turned away whenever they are found not fit to serve the interest of their masters.

Men of large estates would endeavour also to suggest to the most compliant and powerful of their vassals the idea of large farms, that they might have some persons to confide in, to carry on the designs of their ambition. By engrossing farms, and dispossessing families of those appointments which they had shared upon the same tenure, and in common with others in the same situation, it is natural to suppose that the ancient tenants behoved either to be servants to those who were formerly their equals, or seek employment in some other place, and in another condition of life. They could not all be servants to the new engrossers, because they would have no need of them; for it is plain, from experience, that when lands are classed together, and formed systematically, they may be wrought with fewer servants, and at a less expence. What must then have been the consequence? The old country peasants would be obliged to retire to towns, and seek to support their families in some new way.

JAMES MURRAY (1720–1790)

The Cultivation of Holiness

from Small is Beautiful

On a wider view, however, the land is seen as a priceless asset which it is man's task and happiness "to dress and to keep". We can say that man's management of the land must be primarily orientated towards three goals – health, beauty, and permanence. The fourth goal – the only one accepted by the experts – productivity, will then be attained almost as a by-product. The crude materialist view sees agriculture as "essentially directed towards food-production". A wider view sees agriculture as having to fulfil at least three tasks:

- to keep man in touch with living nature, of which he is and remains a highly vulnerable part;
- to humanise and ennoble man's wider habitat; and
- to bring forth the foodstuffs and other materials which are needed for a becoming life.

I do not believe that a civilisation which recognises only the third of these tasks, and which pursues it with such ruthlessness and violence that the other two tasks are not merely neglected but systematically counteracted, has any chance of long-term survival.

ERNST FRIEDRICH SCHUMACHER (1911–1977)

The Land Gift

from Living as the People of God

One practical consequence of this was the unreserved enjoyment of the land as a blessing. Its praises are sung with luxuriant detail in Deuteronomy (*e.g.* 8:7-9; 11:8-12). There was no embarrassment over the prospect of abundant fruitfulness and prosperity. The land was the good gift of their bountiful God and was meant to bring joy, festivity and gratitude. Now of course, as we shall see in a moment, this was contained within a strong moral framework of responsibility to God for one another – especially those who would become poor as a result of corporate disobedience (*cf.* Dt. 15:4ff.). The answer to poverty was not the reduction of all to equivalent frugality, but rather, a return to repentant obedience to God that would raise all to renewed blessing and bounty.

Fourthly, it was the historical land-gift tradition which generated *individual property rights* in Israel. We have already caught a passing glimpse of this in the harvest declaration quoted above. The Israelite farmer speaks of "the firstfruits of the soil that you, O LORD, have given me". Not, we take note, "to us", but "to *me*". The Israelite did not think only in terms of the whole land given to the whole nation. That concept could have been compatible with the whole land being held on the nation's behalf, as it were, by a king as their representative. That, in fact, was the Canaanite system. But such a notion was strongly resisted among the Israelites. The gift of land "percolated", so to speak, down to the lowest social level, so that each individual household could claim that its right to the land it possessed was guaranteed by God himself. Thus, inheritance language was used of the small portions of land belonging to each household, as well as of the territory of whole tribes or the whole nation. They, too, were held as the gift of God.

CHRISTOPHER WRIGHT (1947–)

Enclosure

Far spread the moory ground, a level scene
Bespread with rush and one eternal green,
That never felt the rage of blundering plough,
Though centuries wreathed spring blossoms on its brow
Autumn met plains that stretched them far away
In unchecked shadows of green, brown, and grey.
Unbounded freedom ruled the wandering scene;
No fence of ownership crept in between
To hide the prospect from the gazing eye;
Its only bondage was the circling sky.
A mighty flat, undwarfed by bush and tree,
Spread its faint shadow of immensity,
And lost itself, which seemed to eke its bounds,
In the blue mist the horizon's edge surrounds.

Now this sweet vision of my boyish hours,
Free as spring clouds and wild as forest flowers,
Is faded all –
A hope that blossomed free,
And hath been once as it no more shall be.
Enclosure came, and trampled on the grave
Of labour's rights, and left the poor a slave;
And memory's pride, ere want to wealth did bow,
Is both the shadow and the substance now.
The sheep and cows were free to range as then
Where change might prompt, nor felt the bonds of men.
Cows went and came with every morn and night
To the wild pasture as their common right;
And sheep, unfolded with the rising sun,
Heard the swains shout and felt their freedom won,
Tracked the red fallow field and heath and plain,
Or sought the brook to drink, and roamed again;
While the glad shepherd traced their tracks along,
Free as the lark and happy as her song.

But now all's fled, and flats of many a dye
That seemed to lengthen with the following eye,
Moors losing from the sight, far, smooth, and blea,
Where swopt the plover in its pleasure free,
Are banished now with heaths once wild and gay
As poet's visions of life's early day.
Like mighty giants of their limbs bereft,
The skybound wastes in mangled garbs are left,
Fence meeting fence in owner's little bounds
Of field and meadow, large as garden-grounds,
In little parcels little minds to please,
With men and flocks imprisoned, ill at ease.
For with the poor scared freedom bade farewell,
And fortune-hunters totter where they fell;
They dreamed of riches in the rebel scheme
And find too truly that they did but dream.

JOHN CLARE (1793–1864)

Peasant Technique

from Food First

In dramatic contrast to cash-cropping monoculture, the traditional self-provisioning agriculture that it replaces is often quite sound ecologically. It is a long-evolved adaptation to tropical soil and climate. It reflects a sophisticated understanding of the complex rhythms of the local ecosystem. The mixing of crops, sometimes of more than twenty different species, means harvests are staggered and provides maximum security against wholesale losses due to unseasonable weather, pests, or disease. Moreover, mixed cropping provides the soil with year-round protection from the sun and rain.

The problem of soil erosion *is* serious. But soil erosion occurs largely because fertile land is monopolized by a few, forcing the majority of farmers to overuse vulnerable soils. Moreover, soil impoverishment results, not from an effort to meet the basic food needs of expanding populations, but increasingly from the pressure to grow continuously non-food and luxury export crops over large areas to the neglect of traditional techniques that once protected the soil.

FRANCES MOORE LAPPE

Benefit of Allotments

from The Parson and the Victorian Parish

In the country the vicar might help the poor by finding them allotments, perhaps on the glebe, but if he did this he was advised to make sure that certain conditions were first fulfilled. He must see to it that the local farmers had no objection to the scheme, and it was possible to achieve this if the amount of land made available for an allotment did not exceed what the holder of it, together with his family, could cultivate thoroughly with spade husbandry in their unoccupied and leisure hours. A rood was generally regarded as about the right amount of land if this requirement were to be met, and the land should be let at the same rate as it would be to a farmer, so that farmers could not complain of being treated less fairly than their workers. The creation of allotments, it was maintained, diminished drunkenness, made parishioners happier and more industrious, and helped them to climb several rungs of the social ladder if they showed prowess at cultivation. On light evenings, Flora Thompson recalled, the men, after a hard day's work in the fields and their tea-cum-supper in their cottages, would work strenuously in their gardens and allotments, while on moonlit nights in the spring the solitary fork of someone who had not been able to tear himself away from his land would be heard, and the man singing. The cottage gardens were kept for green vegetables and the pig; the allotments were usually divided into two and used, the one half for potatoes, the other for wheat or barley. If the land were glebe land, then the incumbent could insist that the tenant and his family attend divine service on Sundays and that they should on no account work on the land on that day. If the tenant were convicted of poaching, thieving, drunkenness, or any offence against the laws of the country, he must give up his lot at the Michaelmas ensuing. What spectacle so delightful, asked the Rev. John Sandford, 'as that of a healthy, industrious, contented, and religious peasantry – men civilised and attached by the influence of kindness – whom you found rude, lawless and estranged, because neglected – but whom the sympathy of the superior has reformed and won; and who, instead of being a ready prey to the incendiary and the democrat, are the cheap and loyal defence of property and law?'

PETER HAMMOND

Benefit of Hand Labour

We who seek after the heights of perfection by giving our will to God in a life dedicated to the pursuit of holiness, must, above all, keep charity in our mind's eye as the goal of our endeavour. Charity draws us to God. Charity makes us cleave to God by conforming us to Him. In charity all the fullness of perfection is contained. It is the end towards which we strive, and to which all our life must be directed. And with this aim always in mind, we must travel the road laid down for us by our rule or profession, with a good heart. The things that help us on our way are abstinence, vigils, meditating on God's word, and working with our hands. And if any of these helps is omitted or dispensed, doing damage instead of good service to charity, then the one who is allowed to make dispensations must so arrange things that charity be not made to suffer because of the dispensations he allows. All concerned must be reminded that charity comes first. The superior must see to it that only extreme necessity is allowed as an excuse for setting aside what the rule lays down. Otherwise dispensation becomes something more like destruction. At certain times, certain points of the rule may be modified, according to the needs of everyone's state of health, bodily or spiritual. This is exactly what Saint Benedict says in respect of manual labour. 'Let him (the abbot) order and arrange things with the salvation of his monks' souls in mind. Whatever the brethren do must be done without grumbling. Let everything be done in moderation, for the sake of the weaker brethren.' He does not say that anything is to be totally neglected or set aside on their account. Far from it; he stipulates, in fact, that not even the sick and feeble should be left in idleness, even though they are exempt from heavy work. They are to be given some work that they are capable of doing. No one is entirely exempt from work. The due measure to be observed here is that any one point that raises a particular difficulty is to be dispensed so that all the other points may be better safeguarded, and the point in which anyone thus dispensed most excels can be concentrated on with particular vigour.

AELRED OF RIEVAULX (1109–1167)

Kinship with the Soil

from A Word in Season

When the spent soil of summer yields to the turning blade
and the loose earth rolling tumbles in soft brown disarray,
a ground-swell in the garden recoils along the spade,
a gasp of glad relief quickening the stifled clay,
inspiring a soundless ecstasy of celebration.

I draw involuntary breath,
greeting with empathy this autumn resurrection,
the rescuing flood of light and air dissolving death,
rejuvenating all with thrill of expectation.

My palm I sprinkle with the earthy crumbs of power,
knowing here lies the most unlikely alchemy whence spring
a world of trees and heathered hills, fern, grass and flower,
the unpretentious cradle of green-growing everything.

I breathe upon my palm,
enacting in this deed my kinship with the soil,
sensing the ancient plain-song of the primal psalm
of ground-swell in the garden and God-swell in the soul.

J. EMRYS DAVIES

Free Servitude

                        And then, that evening
Late in the summer the strange horses came.
We heard a distant tapping on the road,
A deepening drumming; it stopped, went on again
And at the corner changed to hollow thunder.
We saw the heads
Like a wild wave charging and were afraid.
We had sold our horses in our fathers' time
To buy new tractors. Now they were strange to us
As fabulous steeds set on an ancient shield
Or illustrations in a book of knights.
We did not dare go near them. Yet they waited,
Stubborn and shy, as if they had been sent
By an old command to find our whereabouts
And that long-lost archaic companionship.
In the first moment we had never a thought
That they were creatures to be owned and used.
Among them were some half-a-dozen colts
Dropped in some wilderness of the broken world,
Yet new as if they had come from their own Eden.
Since then they have pulled our ploughs and borne our loads
But that free servitude still can pierce our hearts.
Our life is changed; their coming our beginning.

EDWIN MUIR (1887–1958)

241

The End of it All

The End of it All

I was once being shown round a rather beautiful garden with a stream running through it and many luxuriant bamboos. The owner who had created it was now a very old man, long retired from a Harley Street practice. As we walked round he made a remark that still haunts me. "You know," he said, "life is a terribly long thing." There was something without hope in his way of saying it. A sense of going on without end while interest faded. In some of the passages already quoted people have spoken of such a lack of purpose or meaning. Others have had visions which pointed them beyond the present and proved potent consolations in the trials and sadnesses of life.

The pieces in this final section are I hope all expressive of purpose. They look forward beyond the edge of our normal, sensible, repetitive, comfortable world. There is a preponderance of poetry since poetry is the form that by tradition nails fragments of eternity.

Snowy Mespilus

Christmas 1964

Ought I to apologise,
Amelanchier Canadensis, delicate leaf,
Single example of myriads none may number,
You that transmute the Sun,
You, with touches of scarlet
And glory of gold upon you
That lie here on the grass
Of a golden October –
Ought I to apologise that I sweep you away?

Frail were your white flowers,
Sweet snowy Mespilus of the spring miracle,
Most tender, unobtrusive in quiet purity.
These, I believe, you protected, my leaf.
These, mystically, chlorophyllic, by gift of Sunshine
Transubstantiating a benediction
Yourself sustained.

Rain, the salt earth, the Sun,
The arbitrament of discriminating roots
Deep in the soil, the unanalysable alchemy
Of trace elements too subtle for understanding,
These, I think, your faith translated to life:
These, ignorantly knowing, you understood,
Hypostatising them by simple dedication
Uncritical, obedient, affirmative.
These were your nutriment, these sustained you,
These your oblations.

Storms, too, were upon you.
Were there not moments of time,
– Dawn, or the stark of night, a day's torment of drought,

Gusts of the sudden thunder, –
When it was less than certain that you could hold
To the frond that held you, or that the frond itself
Could hold to the branch, or that the branch, in turn
Could hold to the stem?

But now the airs of our little garden are still.
A tortoiseshell
Gold, amber, black, on a dead lavender
Suddenly opens her wings. Beyond the wall
Late apples on old trees in tart acidity
Their scarlet bravely assert: and now, the day
His fallen jewels, ochres and rubies, fired
To flame of gold and crimson, fondly enfolds
In liquid light on emerald outspread.
The seasons pause and change: and silently
The single moment stands, the single leaf
Most gently falls.

Ought I to apologise, small single leaf,
That I sweep you away? This little Robin,
A this-year's Robin, his waistcoat newly achieved,
Who follows closely, perkily, fully assured,
 – Just where you lay, only a moment ago,
He found something he needed.
I do not know what it was.

Nor does he know, perhaps,
 – Bright bird, bright fellow mortal,
Small attentive sprite –
That if you were left to lie with the other debris
Of a departing year, in a damp season,
A dying moment, a gust of December.
We might together be blown down dead
In a draggled corner, smothering
In huddled incubus of impersonal apathies
Young glories that grow.

We should yield place to them without misgiving,
Amelanchier Canadensis, fellow servant
Of the days we belong to.
Stillness is ours, my leaf: for now the frosts
Fall from the sharp unclouded crystal of night
Over our silent garden: and now, unseen,
New glories of innumerable stars unborn
Their benediction prepare.

SIR ARTHUR FFORDE (1900–1985)

A Deeper Communion

from Global Theology

Perhaps we can discover through the delicate interdependence of life on earth the deepest source of life which gives unity and meaning to all life. Its very finitude – its limitedness, fragility, transience – leads us to find something beyond it which is reliable, invulnerable. This can only be the infinite. But the infinite is not something we can grasp or possess, even intellectually. It can be known and trusted, in Buber's language, only as "you", the "eternal you" we can dimly sense in every encounter with an earthly "you". It is inevitably elusive, and our experience of it must also be fragile and transient, but it may be enough to give us the basic confidence in life that we need, at least enough to wean us off the dependence on "things" which has made them into damaging idols.

REX AMBLER (1939–)

Communion of Enemies

Isaiah 11: 1–9

There shall come forth a shoot from the stump of Jesse,
   and a branch shall grow out of his roots.
And the Spirit of the LORD shall rest upon him,
   the spirit of wisdom and understanding,
   the spirit of counsel and might,
   the spirit of knowledge and the fear of the LORD.
And his delight shall be in the fear of the LORD.

He shall not judge by what his eyes see,
   or decide by what his ears hear;
but with righteousness he shall judge the poor,
   and decide with equity for the meek of the earth;
and he shall smite the earth with the rod of his mouth,
   and with the breath of his lips he shall slay the wicked.
Righteousness shall be the girdle of his waist,
   and faithfulness the girdle of his loins.

The wolf shall dwell with the lamb,
   and the leopard shall lie down with the kid,
and the calf and the lion and the fatling together,
   and a little child shall lead them.
The cow and the bear shall feed;
   their young shall lie down together;
   and the lion shall eat straw like the ox.
The suckling child shall play over the hole of the asp,
   and the weaned child shall put his hand on the adder's den.
They shall not hurt or destroy
   in all my holy mountain;
for the earth shall be full of the knowledge of the LORD
   as the waters cover the sea.

A New Thing

Isaiah 43: 15–21

"I am the LORD, your Holy One,
   the Creator of Israel, your King."
Thus says the LORD,
   who makes a way in the sea,
   a path in the mighty waters,
who brings forth chariot and horse,
   army and warrior;
they lie down, they cannot rise,
   they are extinguished, quenched like a wick:
"Remember not the former things,
   nor consider the things of old.
Behold, I am doing a new thing;
   now it springs forth, do you not perceive it?
I will make a way in the wilderness
   and rivers in the desert.
The wild beasts will honour me,
   the jackals and the ostriches;
for I give water in the wilderness,
   rivers in the desert,
to give drink to my chosen people,
   the people whom I formed for myself
   that they might declare my praise."

One Foot in Eden

One foot in Eden still, I stand
And look across the other land.
The world's great day is growing late,
Yet strange these fields that we have planted
So long with crops of love and hate.
Time's handiworks by time are haunted,
And nothing now can separate
The corn and tares compactly grown.
The armorial weed in stillness bound
About the stalk; these are our own.
Evil and good stand thick around
In the fields of charity and sin
Where we shall lead our harvest in.

Yet still from Eden springs the root
As clean as on the starting day.
Time takes the foliage and the fruit
And burns the archetypal leaf
To shapes of terror and of grief
Scattered along the winter way.
But famished field and blackened tree
Bear flowers in Eden never known.
Blossoms of grief and charity
Bloom in these darkened fields alone.
What had Eden ever to say
Of hope and faith and pity and love
Until was buried all its day
And memory found its treasure trove?
Strange blessings never in Paradise
Fall from these beclouded skies.

EDWIN MUIR (1887–1958)

First Fruits

from Earth Keeping

Shivering stalks,
Denuded of a golden harvest
Hold fast to the frozen earth.
Icy, cold winds
Mourn a hollow eulogy
Among the naked ranks.

And underneath,
The source of all bounty
Lies still, unmoved.
a fallow resting place.
The very soul of life
Is no more.

And yet,
The lonely stalks, empty husks
Whisper a battle won.
O grave where is thy victory.
O death thy sting?

In unison
The rustling harbingers
Proclaim their Maker's victory.
Deep from within the languished earth
Sprouts forth
The promised stem of Jesse,
First fruits of the golden harvest.

CATHY PATER

Easter

from Questings

Weaving a world of meaning from the joys
And interactions of a home we screen
Ourselves from the screaming blank of a cold
And pointless life. One that keeps hurling back
The cry of Jesus from the cross – "My God,
My God, why hast Thou forsaken me?"
The echo of that cry is with us still.

We lie like pebbles smooth upon the beach
Of time; while the historian's eye selects
A ruby, notes a wetted gleam of red
That fools the hunter's eye, but dries to naught;
While the geologist perceives the slow
Relentless trituration pulverize
Those timeless stones to sand, that forms a rock
Again in ceaseless cycles mocking all.
What is man that Thou art mindful of him,
O Lord, what fleeting specks in time are we?

But as we now peer back from the far bank
Of the baptismal river of our youth's
Absorption with self, having walked the plank
Of love, of marriage, of accomplishment
In our careers, we pace an ordered lawn
Beholding morning-glory blooms at dawn.
Each day the spiralling tip ascends, each
Day immaculate flowers form to die.
Generation upon generation.

An endless repetition of splendid
Striving for perfection. Our own children
In the bud, while our youthful visions wilt.

Will the struggle achieve a fertile seed?
Will fruits develop from the tortured stem?
Or, silted by experience in excess,
And inundated by insignificance,
Will they lack the trace element of faith?
Will they, will we, ascend in Easter praise?
Will we at last perceive beyond the grave?
Beyond the chains of time and space we'll raise
Our songs, as Christ does us with love enslave.

HENRY DISNEY (1938–)

O Jerusalem

Matthew 23: 37–39

O Jerusalem, Jerusalem, killing the prophets and stoning those who are sent to you! How often would I have gathered your children together as a hen gathers her brood under her wings, and you would not! Behold, your house is forsaken. And I tell you, you will not see me until you say, "Blessed be he who comes in the name of the Lord."

Easter Morn

Say, earth, why hast thou got thee new attire,
And stick'st thy habit full of daisies red?
Seems that thou dost to some high thought aspire,
And some new-found-out bridegroom mean'st to wed:
Tell me, ye trees, so fresh apparellèd, –
   So never let the spiteful canker waste you,
   So never let the heavens with lightning blast you, –
Why go you now so trimly dressed, or whither haste you?

Answer me, Jordan, why thy crooked tide
So often wanders from his nearest way,
As though some other way thy stream would slide,
And fain salute the place where something lay.
And you, sweet birds that, shaded from the ray,
   Sit carolling and piping grief away,
   The while the lambs to hear you, dance and play,
Tell me, sweet birds, what is it you so fain would say?

And thou, fair spouse of earth, that every year
Gett'st such a numerous issue of thy bride,
How chance thou hotter shin'st, and draw'st more near?
Sure thou somewhere some worthy sight hast spied,
That in one place for joy thou canst not bide:
   And you, dead swallows, that so lively now
   Through the fit air your wingèd passage row,
How could new life into your frozen ashes flow?

Ye primroses and purple violets,
Tell me, why blaze ye from your leavy bed,
And woo men's hands to rent you from your sets,
As though you would somewhere be carried,
With fresh perfumes, and velvets garnishèd?

But ah! I need not ask, 'tis surely so,
You all would to your Saviour's triumphs go,
There would ye all await, and humble homage do.

GILES FLETCHER (?1588–1623)

The Closer I Move To Death

Who is the light of old
And air shaped Heaven where souls grow wild
　　As horses in the foam:
Oh, let me midlife mourn by the shrined
　　And druid herons' vows
The voyage to ruin I must run,
　　Dawn ships clouted aground,
Yet, though I cry with tumbledown tongue,
　　Count my blessings aloud:

Four elements and five
Senses, and a man a spirit in love
　　Tangling through this spun slime
To his nimbus bell cool kingdom come
　　And the lost, moonshine domes,
And the sea that hides his secret selves
　　Deep in its black, base bones,
Lulling of spheres in the seashell flesh,
　　And this last blessing most,

That the closer I move
To death, one man through his sundered hulks,
　　The louder the sun blooms
And the tusked, ramshackling sea exults;
　　And every wave of the way
And gale I tackle, the whole world then,
　　With more triumphant faith
Than ever was since the world was said,
　　Spins its morning of praise,

I hear the bouncing hills
Grow larked and greener at berry brown
　　Fall and the dew larks sing
Taller this thunderclap spring, and how

More spanned with angels ride
The mansouled fiery islands! Oh,
   Holier than their eyes,
And my shining men no more alone
   As I sail out to die.

DYLAN THOMAS (1914–1953)

The World Transfigured

from Afoot in England

The sun, sinking over the hills towards Swyre and Bridport, turned crimson before it touched the horizon. The sky became luminous; the yellow Chesil Bank, stretching long leagues away, and the hills behind it, changed their colours to violet. The rough sea near the beach glittered like gold; the deep green water, flecked with foam, was mingled with fire; the one boat that remained on it, tossing up and down near the beach, was like a boat of ebony in a glittering fiery sea. A dozen men were drawing up the last net; but when they gathered round to see what they had taken – mackerel or jelly-fish – I cared no longer to look with them. That sudden, wonderful glory which had fallen on the earth and sea had smitten me as well and changed me; and I was like some needy homeless tramp who has found a shilling piece, and, even while he is gloating over it, all at once sees a great treasure before him – glittering gold in heaps, and all rarest sparkling gems, more than he can gather up.

But it is a poor simile. No treasures in gold and gems, though heaped waist-high all about, could produce in the greediest man, hungry for earthly pleasures, a delight, a rapture, equal to mine. For this joy was of another and higher order and very rare, and was a sense of lightness and freedom from all trammels as if the body had become air, essence, energy, or soul, and of union with all visible nature, one with sea and land and the entire vast over-arching sky.

We read of certain saints who were subject to experiences of this kind that they were "snatched up" into some supra-mundane region, and that they stated on their return to earth that it was not lawful for them to speak of the things they had witnessed. The humble naturalist and nature-worshipper can only witness the world glorified – transfigured; what he finds is the important thing. I fancy the mystics would have been nearer the mark if they had said that their experiences during their period of exaltation could not be reported, or that it would be idle to report them, since their questioners lived on the ground and would be quite incapable on account of the mind's limitations of conceiving a state above it and outside of its own experience.

W. H. HUDSON (1841–1922)

Enjoying the World

from Centuries of Meditations

Your enjoyment of the world is never right, till every morning you awake in Heaven; see yourself in your Father's Palace; and look upon the skies, the earth, and the air as Celestial Joys: having such a reverend esteem of all, as if you were among the Angels. The bride of a monarch, in her husband's chamber, hath no such causes of delight as you.

You never enjoy the world aright, till the Sea itself floweth in your veins, till you are clothed with the heavens, and crowned with the stars: and perceive yourself to be the sole heir of the whole world, and more than so, because men are in it who are every one sole heirs as well as you. Till you can sing and rejoice and delight in God, as misers do in gold, and Kings in sceptres, you never enjoy the world.

Till your spirit filleth the whole world, and the stars are your jewels; till you are as familiar with the ways of God in all Ages as with your walk and table: till you are intimately acquainted with that shady nothing out of which the world was made: till you love men so as to desire their happiness, with a thirst equal to the zeal of your own; till you delight in God for being good to all: you never enjoy the world. Till you more feel it than your private estate, and are more present in the hemisphere, considering the glories and the beauties there, than in your own house: Till you remember how lately you were made, and how wonderful it was when you came into it: and more rejoice in the palace of your glory, than if it had been made but to-day morning.

THOMAS TRAHERNE (1637–1674)

Explorations into God

from A Sleep of Prisoners

PETER: The blaze of this fire
  Is wider than any man's imagination
  It goes beyond any stretch of the heart.

MEADOWS: The human heart can go to the lengths of God.
  Dark and cold we may be, but this
  Is no winter now. The frozen misery
  Of centuries breaks, cracks, begins to move;
  The thunder is the thunder of the floes,
  The thaw, the flood, the upstart Spring.
  Thank God our time is now when wrong
  Comes up to face us everywhere,
  Never to leave us till we take
  The longest stride of soul men ever took.
  Affairs are now soul size.
  The enterprise
  Is exploration into God.
  Where are you making for? It takes
  So many thousand years to wake,
  But will you wake for pity's sake?

CHRISTOPHER FRY (1907–)

The Glorious Liberty

Romans 8: 18–25

I consider that the sufferings of this present time are not worth comparing with the glory that is to be revealed to us. For the creation waits with eager longing for the revealing of the sons of God; for the creation was subjected to futility, not of its own will but by the will of him who subjected it in hope; because the creation itself will be set free from its bondage to decay and obtain the glorious liberty of the children of God. We know that the whole creation has been groaning in travail together until now; and not only the creation, but we ourselves, who have the first fruits of the Spirit, groan inwardly as we wait for adoption as sons, the redemption of our bodies. For in this hope we were saved. Now hope that is seen is not hope. For who hopes for what he sees? But if we hope for what we do not see, we wait for it with patience.

Fidelity and Fulfilment

We hardly know in what proportions and under what guise our natural facilities will pass over into the final act of the vision of God. But it can hardly be doubted that, with God's help, it is here below that we give ourselves the eyes and the heart which a final transfiguration will make the organs of a power of adoration, and of a capacity for beatification, particular to each individual man and woman among us.

The masters of the spiritual life incessantly repeat that God wants only souls. To give those words their true value, we must not forget that the human soul, however independently created our philosophy represents it as being, is inseparable, in its birth and in its growth, from the universe into which it is born. In each soul, God loves and partly saves the whole world which that soul sums up in an incommunicable and particular way. But this summing-up, this welding, are not given to us ready-made and complete with the first awakening of consciousness. It is we who, through our own activity, must industriously assemble the widely scattered elements. The labour of seaweed as it concentrates in its tissues the substances scattered, in infinitesimal quantities, throughout the vast layers of the ocean; the industry of bees as they make honey from the juices broadcast in so many flowers – these are but pale images of the ceaseless working-over that all the forces of the universe undergo in us in order to reach the level of spirit.

Thus every man, in the course of his life, must not only show himself obedient and docile. By his fidelity he must build – starting with the most natural territory of his own self – a work, an opus, into which something enters from all the elements of the earth. He makes his own soul throughout all his earthly days; and at the same time he collaborates in another work, in another opus, which infinitely transcends, while at the same time it narrowly determines, the perspectives of his individual achievement: the completing of the world.

PIERRE TEILHARD DE CHARDIN (1881–1955)

A Sign of Eternity

Isaiah 55: 12–13

"For you shall go out in joy,
   and be led forth in peace;
the mountains and the hills before you
   shall break forth into singing,
   and all the trees of the field shall clap their hands.
Instead of the thorn shall come up the cypress;
   instead of the brier shall come up the myrtle;
and it shall be to the LORD for a memorial,
   for an everlasting sign which shall not be cut off."

Thy Kingdom Come

O time to be longed-for, acceptable time, time that every holy man desires daily when he asks in his prayer: "Thy kingdom come, thy will be done on earth as it is in heaven." "All the earth was full of his glory." The earth I walk, I can see; I am aware of the earth I bear with me. There is trouble for both, sighing for both, the anger rather than the glory of God over both. Still the prince of this world reigns over the children of wrath. Daily he rises up against those who believe, and there is scarcely one of the holy ones who does not experience his attacks. Yet "all the earth was full of his glory". And I know that this earth I walk will be delivered from the servitude of corruption, and there will be a new heaven and a new earth, and he who sits on the throne will say: "Behold I make all things new'. The earth I bear with me, too, will be full of the glory of the LORD, though now my earth cries out against me and the flesh lusts against the spirit. "Why are you sad, O my soul, and why do you trouble me?" "Hope in God", for all the earth will be full of his glory. For the present the earth, cursed in the work of Adam, brings me forth thorns and thistles. It is weak and feeble, reluctant and burdensome, subject to so many passions, exposed to so many sicknesses. But "why are you sad, O my soul, and why do you trouble me. All the earth was full of his glory." And when shall this be? When he sits on his throne high and exalted and changes our lowly bodies to be like his glorious body, when that glory which appeared in the Lord's body transfigured on the mount, also appears in our earth, endowed after the resurrection with everlasting life . . . Heaven and earth, the sea and all that is in them, every being, every choice, every movement, every affection, every work, every suffering, every honour, every consolation, every persecution will promote the glory of God, and all things will work together for good to his holy ones. Consider, I beg you, what that joy

269

will be, what singing there will be in our hearts when in God himself we see the causes and reasons for everything that is and will be.

AELRED OF RIEVAULX (1109–1167)

The Final Blessing

from The Assisi Declaration, 1986

But the heart of Christian faith resides in its proclamation of God's merciful fidelity to himself and to the works of his hands. Christians believe that God the Father has not abandoned men and women to their sinful ways but has sent the Saviour to bring redemption and healing to everyone and to all things. Indeed, they firmly confess that Jesus of Nazareth is the Son of God made man, that he is the fulfilment of his Father's covenant with Abraham for the salvation of all peoples and with Noah on behalf of all creation. They maintain that, risen from the dead and ascended into heaven in his glorified humanity, he reconciles all things visible and invisible, and that all creation is therefore purposefully orientated, in and through him, towards the future revelation of the glorious liberty of God's children, when, in the new heavens and the new earth, there will no longer be death, mourning, sadness or pain. Through Christ and through his life-giving Spirit, the Father creates and sanctifies, gives life, blesses and bestows all good things.

Old World Vision

Ezekiel 47: 6–12

And he said to me, "Son of man, have you seen this?"

Then he led me back along the bank of the river. As I went back, I saw upon the bank of the river very many trees on the one side and on the other. And he said to me, "This water flows toward the eastern region and goes down into the Arabah; and when it enters the stagnant waters of the sea, the water will become fresh. And wherever the river goes every living creature which swarms will live, and there will be very many fish; for this water goes there, that the waters of the sea may become fresh; so everything will live where the river goes. Fishermen will stand beside the sea; from En-ge'di to En-eg'laim it will be a place for the spreading of nets; its fish will be of very many kinds, like the fish of the Great Sea.

But its swamps and marshes will not become fresh; they are to be left for salt.

And on the banks, on both sides of the river, there will grow all kinds of trees for food. Their leaves will not wither nor their fruit fail, but they will bear fresh fruit every month, because the water for them flows from the sanctuary. Their fruit will be for food, and their leaves for healing."

The Heavenly Country

Revelation 21: 22–27; 22: 1–5

And I saw no temple in the city, for its temple is the Lord God the Almighty and the Lamb. And the city has no need of sun or moon to shine upon it, for the glory of God is its light, and its lamp is the Lamb. By its light shall the nations walk; and the kings of the earth shall bring their glory into it, and its gates shall never be shut by day – and there shall be no night there; they shall bring into it the glory and the honour of the nations. But nothing unclean shall enter it, nor any one who practises abomination or falsehood, but only those who are written in the Lamb's book of life.

Then he showed me the river of the water of life, bright as crystal, flowing from the throne of God and of the Lamb through the middle of the street of the city; also, on either side of the river, the tree of life with its twelve kinds of fruit, yielding its fruit each month; and the leaves of the tree were for the healing of the nations. There shall no more be anything accursed, but the throne of God and of the Lamb shall be in it, and his servants shall worship him; they shall see his face, and his name shall be on their foreheads.

And night shall be no more; they need no light of lamp or sun, for the Lord God will be their light, and they shall reign for ever and ever.

ACKNOWLEDGEMENTS

The author acknowledges with thanks permission to reproduce the following copyright material:

Rex Ambler: from *Global Theology*, published by SCM Press.

John Arlott: "God whose farm is all creation", reprinted by permission of John Arlott.

Edward A Armstrong: from *St Francis: Nature Mystic*, © 1973, reprinted by permission of The Regents of the University of California.

M K Ashby: from *Joseph Ashby of Tysoe 1859–1919*, published by Merlin Press.

Adrian Bell: from *The Cherry Tree*, published by The Bodley Head, reprinted by permission of the Estate of Adrian Bell.

Martin Buber: from *I and Thou*, published by T & T Clark Ltd, Edinburgh.

John Butler: © John Butler 1990.

Mildred Cable and Francesca French: from *The Gobi Desert*, published by Hodder & Stoughton.

Roy Campbell: from *The Serf*, published Ad Donker (Pty) Ltd.

Pierre Teilhard de Chardin: from *Hymn of the Universe* and *Le Milieu Divin*, published by Editions du Seuil.

Jack Clemo: *Christ in the Claypit*, published by ABP & Methuen Ltd.

Alan T Dale: from *Winding Quest*, reprinted by permission of Oxford University Press.

J Emrys Davies: "Autumn" from *A Word in Season*, published by the National Christian Education Council.

Chandran Devanesen: from *Morning, Noon and Night* ed. by John Carden, published by the Church Missionary Society.

Henry Disney: "Easter" first published in *Questings* by Ronald Lambert, published by Chester House Publications, London.

D H Farmer: from *St Hugh of Lincoln*, published by Darton Longman and Todd.

Sir Arthur fforde: © Arthur fforde, lawyer, headmaster and poet.

Christopher Fry: from *A Sleep of Prisoners*, published by Oxford University Press.

Dag Hammerskjöld: from *Markings*, trans. by W H Auden and Leif Sjoberg, reprinted by permission of Faber and Faber Ltd.

Peter C Hammond: from *The Parson and the Victorian Parish*, reprinted by permission of Hodder & Stoughton Ltd.

G S Hendry: from *Theology of Nature*, published by Westminster Press.

Anita Hewett: from *A Word in Season*, published by the National Christian Education Council.

Donald Hilton: from *A Word in Season*, published by the National Christian Education Council.

Stuart Hine: How Great Thou Art © 1953 Stuart K Hine (dcd). Administered worldwide (excl. USA and Continental America) by Thankyou Music, PO Box 75, Eastbourne, East Sussex BN23. Used by permission.

David Jones: from T*he Sleeping Lord and Other Fragments*, reprinted by permission of Faber and Faber Ltd.

William Langland: from *Piers the Ploughman*.

C S Lewis: from *The Horse and His Boy*, reprinted by permission of HarperCollins, and from *The Magician's Nephew*, published by The Bodley Head.

Andrew Linzey: from *Christianity and the Rights of Animals*, published by SPCK, London.

S McDonagh: from *The Greening of the Church*, published by Cassells Publishers Ltd.

Roy McKay: from *John Leonard Wilson Confessor for the Faith*, reprinted by permission of Hodder and Stoughton Ltd.

John Masefield: from *The Everlasting Mercy*, reprinted by permission of the Society of Authors as the literary representative of the Estate of John Masefield.

H J Massingham: from *English Downland, the English Countryside, the English Countryman*, published by B T Batsford Ltd.

George Matheson: from *O Love that wilt not let me go*. ed. Ian Bradley, published by Collins Ltd.

Yehudi Menuhin: Prayer © Yehudi Menuhin.

Thomas Merton: published by the Sheldon Press.

F Moore Lappe: from *Food First*, reprinted by permission of Souvenir Press Ltd.

Edwin Muir: from *Collected Poems of Edwin Muir*, reprinted by permission of Faber and Faber Ltd.

Richard North: from "A Green and Pleasant Land", published by The Times Newspaper Ltd.

Henri J M Nouwen: from *Pray to Live*, Gill & Macmillan Ltd.

Jean Palaisant: from *The Green Guide*.

Herbert Palmer: from *Poems of Today, Third Series*, reprinted by permission of Macmillan and Co.

Cathy Pater: from *Earthkeeping Magazine* by permission of Cathy Pater.

Alan Pater: from *Cry the Beloved Country*, published by Jonathan Cape Ltd, permission of the Estate of Alan Paton.

R S Pine-Coffin: from *Saint Augustine Confessions*, published by Penguin Classics.

Siegfried Sassoon: from *Collected Poems*, published by Faber & Faber Ltd.

E F Schumacher: from *Small is Beautiful*, published by Abacus.

A Schweitzer: from *Civilization and Ethics* and *Out of My Life and Thought*.

Richard Scorer & Arjen Verkaik: from *Spacious Skies*, published by David
& Charles plc.

E T Seton: from *Wild Animals at Home*, published by Hodder & Stoughton.

G B Shaw: *St Joan.*

Martyn Skinner: from *Old Rectory*, published by Michael Russell, new ed.
1984.

Aelred Squire: from *Aelred of Rievaulx*, published by SPCK Ltd.

John Steinbeck: from *The Grapes of Wrath*, published by William Heine-
mann Ltd.

Helmut Thielicke: from *How the World Began*, reprinted by permission of
James Clarke & Co Ltd, Cambridge.

Dylan Thomas: from *Dylan Thomas, The Poems*, reprinted by permission
of the Trustees for the copyright of the late Dylan Thomas.

Keith Thomas: from *Man and the Natural World*, published by permission
of James Clarke & Co Ltd, Cambridge.

R S Thomas: from *Selected Poems.*

Flora Thompson: from *Lark Rise to Candleford*, reprinted by permission
of Oxford University Press.

Evelyn Underhill: from *Mysticism*, published by Methuen Ltd and from
Immanence, published by J M Dent Ltd.

W H Vanstone: from *Love's Endeavour, Love's Expense*, published by
Darton Longman and Todd.

Geoffrey Webb & Walker: from *The Mirror of Charity*, published by
Mowbrays Ltd.

Dorothea Wender: from *Hesiod and Theogony*, published by Penguin
Classics.

T H White: from *The Sword in the Stone*, published by William Collins
Sons and Co.

L P Wilkinson: from *Virgil, the Georgics*, published by Penguin Classics.

Christopher J H Wright: from *Living As the People of God*, published by
Inter-Varsity Press.

Extracts from the Book of Common Prayer of 1662, the rights in which are
vested in the Crown in perpetuity within the United Kingdom, are
reproduced by permission of the Crown's patentee, Cambridge University
Press.

Scripture quotations are taken from the Revised Standard Version of the
Bible, copyright 1946, 1952, 1971 by the Division of Christian Education
of the National Council of the Churches of Christ in the USA and used
by permission, and from the *New English Bible* Second Edition © 1970,
by permission of Oxford and Cambridge University Presses.

While every effort has been made to trace copyright owners, the author and
publishers apologise to anyone whose rights have inadvertently not been
acknowledged. This will be corrected in any reprint.

INDEX OF AUTHORS